S...

'Big powers ~~... ~~~~~~~~y communication
and healing'

Irish News

'Two Worlds at his feet'

Western Mail

'Stunning clairvoyance... superb mediumship'

Psychic News

'Britain's renowned medium
has helped thousands of people
to contact their loved ones
through his nationwide tours'

HELLO! Magazine

'There is no doubting his sincerity
or his honesty'

Girl About Town, London

'Britain's brightest medium...
Power seems to radiate from his fingertips.
These eyes can see beyond the grave'

Daily Star

'It's hard to be sceptical of the psychic world
when a stranger tells you precisely
what you were doing that morning,
and even days before.
I was startled, almost shocked'

Liverpool Echo

**Books
by the same author:**

VISIONS OF ANOTHER WORLD
The Autobiography of a Medium

VOICES FROM HEAVEN
Communion with Another World

IN TOUCH WITH ETERNITY
Contact with Another World

ANGELS BY MY SIDE
The Psychic Life of a Medium

A GIFT OF GOLDEN LIGHT
The Psychic Journeys of a Medium

THE SPIRITUAL KEYS TO THE KINGDOM
A Book of Soul-Guidance for your Life

THE POWER OF YOUR SPIRIT
Develop your Natural Psychic Abilities

**The Spoken Word
recordings by the same author:**

Life After Death
Heal Yourself
4 Meditations
Develop your Mediumship and Psychic Powers
Develop your Healing Powers
4 Visualisations

*For details of our Worldwide Internet and
Mail Order Catalogue Service, see page 384.*

The Power of your Spirit

Develop your Natural
Psychic Abilities

Visionary and Poet
Stephen O'Brien

Voices

PO Box 8, Swansea, United Kingdom, SA1 1BL

'THE POWER OF YOUR SPIRIT'
A VOICES BOOK
ISBN: 0-9536620-6-3

PRINTING HISTORY:
An Original Voices paperback,
first publication in Great Britain 2003

Typeset by *Voices*.

Printed and bound in Great Britain
by Cox and Wyman Ltd.,
Reading, Berkshire.

To those who serve:
may your spirits soar...

About the Author

At the time of writing this book, bestselling author Stephen O'Brien had been a medium, spiritual healer, visionary and poet for nearly thirty years.

Throughout this period of service, people in all parts of the world benefited from receiving his expert guidance, and from following his instruction on a vast array of paranormal subjects: his teachings circled the planet via his bestselling psychic books, the media, and Internet websites.

The quality of his mediumistic demonstrations is universally acclaimed, and his yearly mammoth tours of the United Kingdom afford the public opportunities to witness his remarkable psychic abilities, and to receive survival evidence of the souls of their loved ones after death.

His educational articles have been published in several psychic and spiritual journals, and he has now gathered these together, updated them, and added much new material to their scope for this book, presenting for the first time an invaluable collection of teachings about mediumship, psychic skills, the spiritual healing powers that lie within us, the important laws of the universe, spiritual ethics, the energies of the mind, and a knowledge of the soul's powers, all of which can transform our way of life.

This book concludes with a revealing, and some-times rather poignant, interview with the author.

CONTENTS

PART THREE
Powerful Spiritual Laws and Ethics,
and Understanding the God-Power Within You

PART FOUR
The Power of your Mind and Thought

PART FIVE
The Power of the Word

Important Notes from the Author

Whether you are, or feel you'd like to be, a psychic, a medium, or a spiritual healer, I advise you to read this book in its entirety, for each section contains vital information that all sensitives should know: the teachings encompass many aspects of soul-sensitivity and psychic awareness, from which all branches of your spiritual life and work might benefit.

For example, if you're interested only in healing you'd be unwise to skip Part One's essential guidance: if you ignore this section, you'll miss out on a great deal of important basic training.

Millions of people today accept the reality of an afterlife, and there is available a vast body of evidence which supports our knowledge of individual survival after death; so, I'll not be adding to it: instead, I'll be concentrating on how you can obtain it for yourself.

I continue to receive letters from people around the world who wish to develop their natural psychic skills but cannot find a sensible tutor to guide them through the maze of laws and the 'unwritten codes of conduct' and pitfalls that they might encounter while trying to unfold their sensitivity.

I hope this book will meet some of these needs.

Although no one can be changed into a deeply sensitive being simply by reading a book, knowledge is priceless – and knowledge will empower you.

Some readers might be surprised to find in the later sections of this book the subjects of spiritual ethics, morals, and some simple philosophy, but these topics should occupy an important place in the education of any responsible sensitive. All sensitives take upon themselves, either knowingly or unwittingly, the role of educators: they become teachers, shiners of the light of truth; and if you belong within their ranks your mind should be prepared to answer some of the searching questions that the public will undoubtedly ask you.

I wish you well on your journey of self-discovery, and in your quest for spiritual, psychic and mental progression.

I can confidently predict that it won't be an easy pathway for you, for the way of service never is – but it can be an exciting and spiritually satisfying adventure.

May your light shine brightly.

Stephen O'Brien
'Willowtrees Cottage'
Wales, August 2003

PART ONE

Developing your Psychic, Mediumistic, and Spiritual Healing Powers

1

Preparation for Development
Sensitives and their Motivation

Why do you want to develop your natural psychic abilities? Why do you want to be a medium, a spiritual healer, or a psychic sensitive?

It's vitally important that you fully understand your true motivation for undertaking any psychic- or soul-development *before* any experimentation takes place, because of the following unbreakable Universal Law which should be impressed forever in your mind:

Like Attracts Like.

This important esoteric law will ensure from the start of your development that from the worlds of spirit (as well as from this earthly plane of thought) you will draw to yourself the help only of similarly motivated people.

Your mind, your character, and your true state of soul-evolution are your inner strength: they are your unshakeable shield and protection; and you should also be aware that from the start of your journey you must *earn* every word of the wise spiritual guidance you desire, and that this can be achieved only through sustained personal effort.

Remember, too, that the spirit people you have

quite naturally attracted to yourself through the law of *Like Attracts Like* already know you much better than you know yourself.

Evolved spirit guides and communicators in the next world can read your mind quite easily: your thoughts are an open book to them.

What kind of character qualities, then, should you be aiming to encourage in yourself, and what kinds of traits should you be trying to eradicate from your personality in order to attract the best kind of spiritual guidance and help?

Aspirants who are deceitful, uncaring, aggressive, arrogant, supercilious, unintelligent, ignorant, unkind, mean or self-centred, and in whose heart there is little or no love for humanity or for the animal kingdom, or for the Mother Planet upon which we all dwell, will undoubtedly attract to themselves discarnate personalities who are existing (or vibrating) at roughly the same stage of evolution as themselves.

'Birds of a feather, flock together', which is why you should try to be a compassionate and loving individual.

If you are a compulsive liar who deceives others in order to achieve your own desires, you can expect nothing but similar treatment from your inspirers in the next world.

If you show no love or genuine concern for the welfare of humanity or the animal kingdom, or for those who grieve or who are in pain, or for those who fear where their lives might be leading them, your inspirers will behave towards you in a similar hard-hearted way.

Idle sensation-seekers, inadequate personalities,

cruel and aggressive people, or people with over-emotional, unbalanced mentalities, or anyone who might be regarded as an unpleasant extremist or an egotist who might be seeking a public platform purely to receive adoration – all of these people should avoid developing their psychic powers.

WARNING and DISCLAIMER: If you possess an unbalanced emotional or mental nature you should avoid developing mediumship or any form of psychic skill because the spirit power-processes involved in this development can excite your nervous system and agitate your thought-patterns. It can also affect the delicate balance of your body's hormonal systems and its endocrine (or ductless gland) structures.

If you have received any form of psychiatric or psychological treatment, or have undergone clinical depression or any other form of mental or emotional illness, which includes drug abuse or alcohol addiction, then do not proceed with any form of psychic or mediumistic development without first seeking approval from your doctors.

Developing your soul-abilities can affect your entire physical, mental, emotional and psychic being, and it is a very serious undertaking – it isn't a light-hearted 'pastime' or a toy to be played with for idle amusement.

I'll state the Law again: *Like Attracts Like*, and I'll add to it another related occult (or 'hidden') Law: *As below, so above.*

Seek, and you will find what you are looking for.

Knock, and the door will be eventually be opened to you.

Just as in the Earthworld, in the spirit world there are discarnate minds of varying degrees of intelligence and of all kinds of moral persuasions.

In the lower 'astral planes', which are the thought-worlds or 'shining worlds' of illusion that vibrate nearest to our Earth, there exist many unevolved inhabitants who are more than willing to communicate much foolish nonsense, which the power of your mentality should drive away.

The myriad Natural Laws of the Universe cannot be cheated or broken; so, when adolescents play at ouija-board séances or hostile sceptics deliberately set out to ridicule genuine mediums, in both instances they achieve the results they desire.

If you would like to receive the highest spiritual teachings and the purest, most reliable guidance, then you must earn it; you must win it by virtue of your sincere thoughts, feelings and intentions.

Centuries ago, this inscription was written over the portals of the Ancient Mystery Temples: *Man Know Thyself.*

In the preparatory stages of development, think seriously about which positive aspects of your character you should try to encourage, and which negative aspects you should try to expunge from your mind, in order to obtain spiritual success.

These characteristics of your 'persona' (or 'mask', which is but a pale reflection of your mind) could fall broadly into two categories, which are:

+ The qualities of the Heart (your emotions)
+ The qualities of the Mind (your mentality)

It is your character that holds the shining jewels of

compassion, consideration, sympathy, empathy, genuine care and concern for all creatures and their environments; and by far the hardest of the spiritual qualities to attain, and then to rigorously maintain, is the powerful quality of Unconditional Love.

Unconditional Love

Unconditional love is not possessive: it isn't a self-rewarding stewardship which gives so that it might later receive; neither does it make unreasonable demands upon others in order to satisfy its possessor's need for pleasure or desire.

Unconditional Love remains steadfast no matter what force or energy tries to shake it. Born of the spirit, it continues to operate beyond all suffering and endurance. Through adversity and throughout the darkness of personal despair, the possessor of unconditional love continues to care for other life-forms, even when called upon to make personal sacrifices.

It is Unconditional love that gives rise to the ethic of Service.

All sensitives should be idealists.

To love unconditionally means that we should never cease to support those who stand in need – even when all hope of any favourable response has long been lost.

This kind of selfless love is best expressed by a truly compassionate mother as she tenderly cares for her child, simply because her child exists: there is never any emotional blackmail involved in this relationship; it's a form of pure love, and there are never any ulterior motives.

Before you undertake any psychic or mediumistic development, think long and hard, and take time to consider this carefully:

Are you capable of giving, or of developing, the beneficent quality of unconditional love?

Search yourself deeply, and be brutally honest with yourself.

With the vibrant flame of compassion burning in your heart (and this, esoterically speaking, is where the love-light frequently manifests) you cannot help but attract from the invisible worlds the help of spiritually evolved personalities, for it is these benevolent influences who are motivated to serve mankind.

I ended my book, *Visions of Another World*, with this truism: *Without Love, we are nothing.*

This single phrase is worthy of your deepest contemplation *before* you embark on any psychic or mediumistic journey of self-discovery.

To bring forth a fruitful and spiritual form of service, in whatever field of sensitivity you choose to operate, you should first learn to know yourself – truly and honestly – and you should become aware of all your glaring faults, as well as of your laudable credits.

You should gain self-knowledge, and not remain in a state of ignorance.

Try to understand the psychology of your mental make-up. Ask your friends to provide objective opinions about your real character.

Discovering what those closest to you *really* think about you could open your eyes, and increase your understanding.

Look carefully into the pictures of your past.

Have you served others in your life? Or have you been unkind and uncaring?

If you've been unkind, then I would strongly advise you to start serving the world unselfishly from today onwards, in any way you can. Into your daily life, build up the habit of rendering selfless service to others. Be kind to them; and you will earn your spiritual reward.

Daily build up your knowledge, for it is from this storehouse of facts, and your ability to correlate them, that wisdom may come.

Knowledge always attracts knowledge, and intelligence reaps its reward.

Read the works of all the respected writers on paranormal subjects; read about the science and art of mediumship and of spiritual healing, and about other esoteric topics and occult sciences. Read widely and intelligently, but never forget to question everything.

A gradual increase of knowledge will banish ignorance from your mind. There should be no place for ignorance in the mind of a psychic sensitive.

Keeping an Open Mind
One further caution here with regard to your beliefs: always keep and open mind on all things. As you travel along the arduous road of spiritual unfoldment your invisible inspirers will doubtless challenge to the uttermost all of your belief-systems, but if you close your mind to their ideas there can be no hope of progress for you.

You must be prepared to have your religious beliefs not only questioned, but also revised and corrected.

Criticise yourself first *before* you turn your attention to others.

And always do your best.

With a loving and willing heart, do your best to serve others.

As we walk along the ancient pathway of psychic and spiritual unfoldment, there is always more to discover about the hidden psychic nature of man, the natural laws that govern spirit communication, mental attunement, thought and prayer, spirit guides and spiritual healing, and psychic reception and transmission faculties.

We shall touch upon all of these topics, and many more, such as how to form a properly-conducted soul-awareness group or psychic development class.

If you remain undaunted by what you've read so far, and you still want to be a psychic sensitive, from today onwards start putting into practice all of the above suggestions; and be aware that as you deepen your sensitivity, you will heighten your awareness of the good side of your nature and of the less attractive side, too.

Be prepared to be challenged.

Now let's take a critical look at the 'gifts' of the spirit, and discover how you can safely develop them.

2

Acquiring Knowledge

Caution: If you skipped the first chapter of this book, which deals with your motivation and some important Universal Laws, exercise self-discipline now, and turn back the pages and read it before you proceed further.

There's a great deal of essential advice in that chapter, which also contains serious warnings about the dangers you might encounter if you remain ignorant of some of the Universal Laws that govern the unfoldment of your sensitivity.

Every one of God's creations possesses psychic power: the word *Psyche* comes from the Greek language and broadly translates as *Soul*.

Psychic Powers are Soul Powers.

We each have a soul and therefore each one of us is psychic, but in some people this natural ability seems more developed and unfolded, while in others it seems to lie quite dormant or is only just awakening.

But let me state, right here at the beginning, that genuine mediums, psychics and spiritual healers of outstanding ability are rare beings indeed. Yes, we all have the potential within us; yes, we can all develop these skills to the best of our abilities, but

STEPHEN O'BRIEN

not many of us will attain mastery of them. We can
all learn to play the piano, but how many of us will
excel in this art and become concert pianists?

And even fewer of us are likely to become master
composers. Nevertheless, we can try to achieve our
own highest standard of work.

Indications of Sensitivity

At some time in their lives, most people experience
some kind of psychic 'happening' and this might
include any of the following occurrences, which
indicate the presence of latent psychic sensitivity:

♦ Turning around quickly in a public place and
  pinpointing someone who's been staring at the
  back of your head.
♦ Sensing pleasant or unpleasant atmospheres in
  buildings, or around certain people.
♦ Being aware of the true characters of people.
♦ Sensing that 'someone' is watching over you or
  observing you; or getting strong feelings that
  you're not alone.
♦ Having 'hunches' that come true, or exercising
  'Feminine Intuition'.
♦ Thinking about someone you haven't seen for a
  long time, and then you bump into them.
♦ Knowing who's on the other end of the phone
  before you answer it.
♦ Holding a photograph of someone you don't
  know, but being aware of his or her personality.
♦ Having feelings about the future, about what
  might happen.
♦ Seeing small objects move of their own accord
  in your presence.
♦ Being vaguely aware of invisible 'energy-fields'

24

or sensing 'colours' around people.

+ Reading the tea-leaves or playing-cards for fun,
  but achieving a degree of accuracy.
+ Playing with an invisible playmate when you
  were a child.
+ Seeing a ghost, or shadowy forms out of the
  corner of your eye.
+ Seeing 'lights' in your bedroom at night.
+ Having presentiments or psychics warnings;
  'knowing' that something unpleasant might
  happen.
+ Dreaming about loved ones who've died, and
  holding conversations with them.
+ Guessing what the contents of a letter are,
  before you open it.
+ Hearing a spirit-voice calling your name, or
  hearing 'someone' speak to you when you least
  expect it.
+ 'Flying' in the Astral World at night, when
  you're freed from your physical body.
+ Knowing you have a sixth-sense; and sometimes experiencing a sense of foreboding.
+ Having an out-of-the-body experience (known
  as an OOBE); or a near-death experience (an
  NDE).

Even if you haven't had any of these experiences,
your soul-faculties can still be awakened and
developed.

Having already discussed what a sensitive's true
motivation for undertaking psychic or mediumistic
development should be, and assuming that you've
started putting into practice what you learned from
your basic character self-analysis, we can now
move forward.

How do you unfold your 'gifts of the spirit'? And where can you go to receive help?

'Is it a Gift, or is it a Skill?'

The 'gifts' of the spirit are also 'skills'.

Your soul-powers are natural abilities which you must rediscover, try to fully understand, diligently unfold, and then strengthen until they come under your mental control.

The 'gift' of sensitivity is often believed to be inherited from 'gifted' ancestors, but everyone has psychic abilities. No one can give you the 'gift' of **clairvoyance** (which translates from French as *clear-seeing*), or **clairaudience** (*clear-hearing*), or **clairsentience** (*clear-sensing*): you already possess these natural abilities, albeit in embryonic form; but you are responsible for unfolding and refining these soul-powers.

Many sensitives believe that God gives us the gifts, but it's up to us to develop them.

Are mediums born or are they made?

To answer this question, and other issues it raises, here is my spirit guide who, when on Earth, was a Native American Indian known as White Owl:

Where any form of mediumship is evident, you can be sure that its possessor has earned every jot of that facility through hard work in prior incarnations.

Mediumship functions more favourably through certain physical bodies because of their chemical make-up, which is why the incarnating servant selects a suitable family group, and personally decides on his own destiny and broad future upbringing, before his life materialises on Earth.

Mediums are born with a mission, to play their part in the Divine Scheme of things.

Mediums have a sacred calling — but, if you are a public medium, I have a question for you: *what exactly are you doing*? You are most certainly *not* proving survival of the human soul after death: some of the best scientific minds in your world, and in mine, would find it extremely difficult to prove that you are now existing in *your* world, not to mention in mine.

Ultimate proof of survival comes when you pass from the Earth and arrive in my world. Then there is no doubt about your eternal nature.

Mediums are providing *evidence* of survival, but not proof *per se*. They are offering a priceless service to those who feel spiritually lost: to the lonely and the ignorant, and to those who mourn and who need knowledge of spiritual realities.

They are comforters and educators.

Those who are serving in this way chose this time to undertake their current responsibilities — it is all impressed within your spiritual nature, in your pathway; and there are far deeper implications to being a living entity who claims conscious links to us than at first might be imagined.

Mediums should not deceive themselves as to their true role in the Divine Plan.

Finding a Tutor

Knowledge should always be embraced, and there are a number of places where you can receive tuition, but whichever place you choose do take your full quota of intelligence along with you, and all of your reasoning power, as well as your ability to be completely honest with yourself and others – and don't forget you'll also need a deep thirst for knowledge and a heart so full of love for humanity that it overflows.

If you possess these worthy qualities, then be assured that this ancient law will operate: *'When the pupil is ready, the master will appear'*.

The onus is on you, the pupil, to attract the master's presence: you will have to earn the right to receive your spiritual instruction by developing your spiritual nature.

And here's a further word of caution: when you're choosing your earthly tutor, take great care – anyone can claim to train sensitives (I've met many such 'teachers') but this doesn't mean they know what they're doing. Few people understand the true psychic and spiritual nature of man, that he's a triune being, comprising body, mind and spirit.

The teachers are many, but the wise are few.

Choose your tutor carefully because 'When the blind lead the blind, they will both fall into the ditch'.

Use your inner Psychic Awareness, your natural sense of ESP (Extra Sensory Perception), or your innate Intuition wisely, and in prayerful silence earnestly seek the assistance of higher authorities to guide you to the right person, remembering always that you'll attract only those who are in attunement with your mental frequencies and soul-evolution vibrations.

For this reason, you should be clear in your mind about what kind of instruction you require.

Decide now; because fortune-tellers and the

often-advertised clairvoyant (or clear-seer), or the palmist and the tarot-card reader cannot train you to become a medium or a spiritual healer, for they are only psychics; they're not mediums.

Psychics don't contact discarnate intelligences: psychics use telepathic powers to read people's minds, characters and the ambient atmospheres that surround them.

If you're seeking a psychic's help, choose wisely: many psychics don't know how to train others because they, themselves, don't understand how their abilities function.

The key qualities to look for in a teacher are education and intelligence.

Good teachers possess many other qualities, of course, but without the benefit of education fuelled by a bright intelligence, they will be poor guides indeed.

If you want to be a medium or a spiritual healer, then search within the Spiritualist Movement, for it's there, or in one of its allied study-groups, societies or kindred psychic associations, that mediums of all shades of mental, emotional, and spiritual development are to be found.

Common sense dictates that if you wish to develop mediumship you should find respected mediums to train you. They can guide, instruct, and support you as you gently unfold your own sensitivity because they've walked the path before you, and they understand the processes involved.

A Warning about Internet Knowledge
At the time of writing, anyone can publish websites on the Internet, and there's a great deal of dubious

material available in cyberspace.

Exercise caution.

Access the websites of national organisations or reputable kindred bodies associated with your subject, and follow the teachings only of well-respected and recognised authorities.

Remember these two important points:

- Famous people don't always make the best teachers.

- Psychically-developed people aren't necessarily spiritually-developed people.

Don't fall into the trap of believing that because someone is psychically gifted he or she must also be a spiritually-developed soul.

This isn't usually the case.

Psychic abilities are mental skills; but spirituality is a character and soul quality that is much harder to attain.

A psychic is merely a psychically-aware person, but a truly spiritual person is a sensitive and great soul, and these beings are rare indeed.

3

The Gifts of the Spirit

As part of the extensive groundwork you should be doing, find time to think carefully about what kinds of psychic or spiritual abilities you would like to develop.

Could you list some of the basic psychic skills, which have nothing to do with contacting the spirit world, but are purely psychic abilities?
Yes I can; and as you'll see, the list is quite long, though not definitive. Take note that none of the following skills requires the sensitive to be in touch with people living in the spirit world.

A Basic List of Psychic Abilities

♦ Psychometry (which broadly translates from Greek as 'a measure of the soul of things').
♦ Telepathy (mind-reading).
♦ Clairvoyance (clear-seeing).
♦ Clairaudience (clear-hearing: it's possible to hear another person's mind-voice).
♦ Clairsentience (clear-sensing).
♦ Feminine Intuition ('hunches').
♦ Telekinesis (movement of physical objects by

your mind-power).

- Flower Clairsentience (the sensing of psychic impressions left upon flowers).
- Sand and ribbon readings (interpreting their shapes or colours).
- Scrying (using a crystal ball, a mirror, or a bowl of clear water).
- Tealeaf reading.
- Reading the tarot or a pack of playing-cards.
- Auric readings.
- Character readings.
- Sensing ghosts, 'presences', or atmospheres in buildings.
- Reading the rune-stones.
- Auric diagnosis (diagnosing health problems, which are seen in the physical aura).
- Prediction (forecasting future possibilities).
- Precognition (seeing the future).
- Visualisation.
- Meditation.
- Psychic self-defence.
- Psychic dreaming.
- Astral travelling (in your etheric double, you can visit the astral worlds of spirit).
- Bi-location (the ability to be seen in two places at the same time).
- Water-divining (locating water – or other substances – by psychic means).
- Healing with crystals; or using a pendulum.
- Magnetic healing (sharing your own psychic energies with sufferers).
- Out-of-the-Body Experiences (OOBEs).
- Near Death Experiences (NDEs).
- Discovering previous lives (or viewing what are known as the Akashic Records).

Could you also provide a basic list of mediumistic abilities?
Yes.

Different forms of mediumship can be developed and these fall into two categories: Mental and Physical Mediumship abilities.

Take note that *all* of the following skills definitely require the sensitive to be in touch with people who are living in the world of spirit.

A Basic List of Mental and Physical Mediumship Abilities

Mental Mediumship
Some of the main mental skills are:

♦ Communication with people in the spirit world (message relaying: the seeing, hearing and sensing of spirit world inhabitants).
♦ Inspirational speaking and writing (serving as a medium or agent for discarnate intelligences).
♦ Trance (when you allow a discarnate person to 'overshadow' your thought-processes, ranging in depth from a light and almost imperceptible link of inspiration, to a seemingly cataleptic state in which mediums claim they have no knowledge of what transpires).
♦ Zenoglossy (speaking in an authentic foreign language that is presently unknown to you).
♦ Psychic Portraiture (sometimes called Psychic Art, in which the medium draws the faces of the deceased: this skill may also require a small amount of physical mediumship ability).

Physical Mediumship

Some of the main abilities associated with physical mediumship are:

♦ Spiritual Healing (the results of which are often physical: cancerous growths might be reduced or dispersed, or bone deformities might be straightened etc. But the medium also requires a clear state of mental attunement with the spirit world before any spiritual healing can take place).

♦ Automatic Writing (when control is taken of the medium's hand in order to deliver written communications).

♦ Ouija-board communications (achieved by means of an alphabet-board and a glass or pointer, which are operated by discarnates when the board is used correctly).

♦ Planchette (a wooden device with a pencil through it, with which spirit communicators write their messages).

♦ Table-titling (in its most efficient form).

♦ Spirit photography (or thought-ography; when spirit faces or thought-images are impressed on photographic film).

♦ Psychic Portraiture.

♦ Transfiguration (when faces of spirit people are physically 'built up' over the bone-structure of a medium's face).

♦ Materialisation (when spirit people 'clothe' themselves in temporary physical bodies).

♦ Levitation or Telekinesis (the movement of physical objects, including people).

♦ Direct Voice Phenomena (when voices of the

'dead' vibrate our atmosphere through an ectoplasmic voice-box that is created by spirit operators from specialised energies withdrawn from the medium, sitters and the séance-room fabrics).

Study specialist books on the above subjects until you gain a reliable understanding of all these soul faculties and how they work. Never be ignorant.

And remember that progress won't come quickly. In all matters pertaining to the spirit, unfoldment is always a gradual step-by-step process.

In our modern technological society, which has instant coffee, instant Internet access, and instant 'cures' are sold over the counter, you may be certain of this:

There can be no instant mediumship; there can be no immediate psychic or spiritual mastery.

Psychic development, by its very nature, is a gradual process.

A human foetus inside its mother's womb takes approximately nine months to form, according to a process governed by Natural Law.

In the animal kingdom, a baby chick will develop inside its egg and peck its way out into freedom only when the time is right: if its protective shell is broken too soon, disaster may result.

Many aspiring sensitives are far too eager and all too willing to jump onto the public platform long before their abilities and psychic powers have been sufficiently developed and properly balanced; and regrettably, there will always be ignorant folk who will be more than happy to book their services.

To be a true initiate you must have patience.

You must be trusting; and you should cultivate a high degree of self-discipline and self-control, and also build up within you a storehouse of spiritual understanding.

If you can then find a warm and harmonious home-circle in which to develop your abilities, or a Spiritualist Church psychic development class, or a private awareness group to accept you as a student – you may consider yourself fortunate, indeed. Many Spiritualist teachers and respected mediums or psychics regularly turn away dozens of aspirants, stipulating that each applicant must first be well known to the tutor before he is allowed access into their circles. (And quite rightly so.)

*

Would you give us your definition of what a mental medium is?
A mental medium is a person who links his mind with the minds of discarnate intelligences, and then endeavours to relay their messages to their loved ones, friends, or relatives living on the Earth.

Would you give us your definition of what a physical medium is?
A physical medium is a person whose physical and soul-energies are drawn upon by people in the next world so that they might communicate with their loved ones here on the Earth. The special energies provided by physical mediums are used by their spirit co-operators to create temporary physical bodies, or hands or faces, or voice-boxes through which discarnates may make themselves known in

our material world. Physical mediumship is a specialised form of communication, and one in which the health of the medium can be adversely affected if some very strict guidelines are ignored.

In materialisation circles, spirit guides claim that they draw upon many vibrating energy-fields in and around the séance-room in order to create physical phenomena: they withdraw energies from the furniture, carpets and fixtures in the séance-room, as well as from the personal soul-energy fields of the sitters.

They've even been known to colour spirit visitors' garments with dyes 'borrowed' from séance-room fabrics.

Do mental mediums use psychic powers to obtain their links with the Other Side?
Yes. A mental medium tries to focus the beam of his psychic awareness into the realms of spirit, in an effort to see, hear, or sense the people living there.

Do mediums work exclusively with the spirit world, or can some psychic impressions creep into their messages?
No medium can work exclusively with the spirit people: a degree of telepathic information will always reach him from his sitters' minds.

All mediums are psychic – but not all psychics are mediums.

Read that statement again, and think about it until you can fully appreciate its meaning and implications. Very few mediums sift through the many impressions that reach them from both worlds, and then present from these some excellent mediumistic messages.

The solution to the distressing problem of how to raise the standards of mediumship rests with the mediums themselves.

All mediums have a responsibility to educate themselves and to obtain sensible training from wise teachers, and not to allow themselves to be led astray by ignorance and foolishness.

During their years of service, all sensitives should strive to continually improve the quality of their work. They should tape their services and carefully analyse them afterwards; and they should seek out and always welcome criticism, which should then be examined objectively. Both constructive and so-called destructive comments can, and certainly do, help sensitives to improve their skills.

I'm confused. I've heard recipients receiving through mediums the registration numbers of their cars, their phone numbers and addresses, and even their own initials. Was this information gained psychically, or mediumistically?
Always apply a good dose of common sense to these problems.

What on earth would be the point of a spirit communicator telling you where you live, or confirming your car registration number? You already know where you live, and what's written on your numberplate.

There's very little meaningfulness behind this kind of communication: it isn't spiritually comforting or encouraging (though it can be startling and impressive); and hearing these kinds of details won't mend your broken heart, or place you in contact with someone you've loved and seemingly 'lost'. Neither will cold facts and figures spiritually change your life; although they might make you think differently.

There's nothing wrong with mediums relaying stark, factual evidence: it has its rightful place, and public displays of clairvoyance should always contain a good deal of this information, but the medium who gives this type of emotionless and spiritually 'empty' message has probably gleaned the facts from his sitter's mind, and not from the mind of a spirit communicator.

The mediumship would be more likely to be judged genuine if the medium were to correctly relay the *communicator's* name and earth address, and *his* old car registration number.

Could you highlight more clearly for us an example of the differences between a psychic and a mediumistic message?

Yes, I can.

Let's suppose a sensitive says to you, 'I see the name of Jack; and... you have a bad leg that hurts a lot; and you've been buying some red shoes.'

These are cold statements of fact, simple psychic impressions that have been gleaned telepathically from your mind: they contain no evidence of a compassionate invisible entity who's trying to communicate his presence and personality to you.

This message is all about *you*: it contains your own memories, and outlines your own aches and pains and your own actions; but none of these details tells us anything about 'Jack', the supposed spirit communicator – you are told nothing about *his* memories or *his* emotions.

The next time a medium gives you a string of information like this, ask him, 'Who is this Jack you're speaking about? Can you identify him; and what is his reason for contacting me?'

I've often felt disappointed with the work of many mediums: to me they seem to be nothing more than clever telepaths, or deluded exhibitionists craving a captive audience. What can be done to improve matters?
You can use your voice to vigorously complain to the people who book these under-developed sensitives, and try to remove them from public view. You could start a clean-up campaign; you could discuss these ideas at Spiritualist church circles, psychic societies, or in private groups and classes.

But you won't be popular, for no reformer has ever escaped the wrath of the establishment.

My own view is clear: undeveloped sensitives should find no place on the public platform: they should go back into the development class to be properly trained.

What characteristics would you say mark out a genuine mediumistic message?
All mediumistic messages must contain sufficient evidence which points to the presence of a spirit communicator, who should also state the reason why he's making contact with us.

I shall examine this subject in greater depth, later in the book.

40

At this point, you're probably brimming with many more questions such as:

If I can't find a good circle, can I start my own class?

I'm already in a group, but how do I know it's being run correctly?

How can I tell if the methods employed by my teacher will produce satisfactory results?

Patience is a virtue.

We shall address all of these issues in due course; but first, you'll need some important knowledge about your 'hidden' psychic make-up.

4

The Chakras:
Your Psychic Energy-Centres

Before unfolding your sensitivity, you should have a basic understanding of your psychic apparatus.

The Seven Main Psychic Centres or Chakras
Mediums and spiritual healers aren't contacted by the spirit world through their clumsy, slow physical senses, but rather through their minds via their etheric (or spirit) bodies; and psychics also receive paranormal information through this same 'hidden' psychic apparatus.

We each possess a set of inner soul bodies which have, built within them, hundreds of sensitive life-energy receptors and transmitters.

These high-frequency etheric structures have been called the Psychic Centres or the Chakras, and it is through these, as well as through the mind, that psychic impressions and other subtle spirit-energies reach us.

Chakra is an old Sanskrit word which translates broadly as a 'wheel', and many clairvoyants have described seeing the chakras as whirlpools of radiant colour and energy, situated on, within, and through the etheric bodies of man.

Most schools of thought agree that there are seven main chakras or psychic centres, but some claim there are thousands more.

The chakras play a far more important role in our lives than simply that of being the means through which spirit communication and other psychic impressions reach us.

The chakras are our life-line links to the Source of All Power, or to God, the Great Spirit.

Pouring through these psychic portals comes the very Life-Force or Spark of the Divine Spirit which vitalises us, and it has a profound effect on all levels of our being. Eastern races termed this form of life-energy *Prana*. Limited space doesn't permit a full discussion of the many complexities of the chakra-system here, so I will concentrate on only four of the centres – those over the solar-plexus, the throat, the brow, and the crown, all of which play important roles in the development of any psychic, mediumistic or spiritual healing abilities.

All the chakras link up to nerve-complexes in the body, and the locations of the seven main chakras, or psychic energy-centres, are listed beneath (see the illustration), with their basic psychic functions, followed by the glands in the body to which many sensitives believe they're linked.

1. At the base of the spine: there is a centre called the root or base chakra, which is a main point of entry through which the powerful cosmic life-force energises the bodies of man. (Gonads.)
2. Over the sexual organs (in the groin): there is the sacral centre which is closely linked to the procreative energies. (Gonads/Lymphatics.)

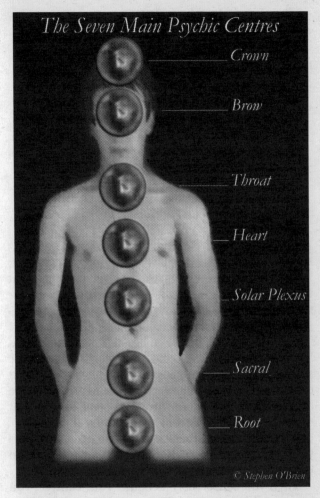

The Seven Main Psychic Centres

Crown

Brow

Throat

Heart

Solar Plexus

Sacral

Root

© Stephen O'Brien

3. Over the solar plexus (situated between the end of the breastbone and just above the navel): there is a centre which registers sensation, feeling and

emotion. (Adrenal glands.)

4. Over the heart: there is a centre that registers deep-seated emotions. (Thymus gland.)

5. Over the throat: there is a centre that registers the reception and transmission of psychic sound-waves. (Thyroid gland.)

6. In the centre of the head (above the eyebrows): there is a centre that registers impressions of sight, visualisation, and mental image-making. (Pituitary gland.)

7. In the centre of the head (on the top of the skull): there is a centre that registers thought-reception and transmission, and it also links man to the Cosmic Life Force. (Pineal gland.)

A little study will clearly reveal what impressions may reach you through each point of contact; however, it's interesting to note, in passing, that many students are surprised to learn that we hear the spirit people's voices across the throat chakra-point, via the aural centre.

Much nonsense is spoken about 'opening up' and 'closing-down' these chakras after any psychic activity. Your psychic centres are always open: if ever they were to close, you would cease to be alive. What some ill-informed teachers might mean when they instruct their pupils to 'open-up' or to 'close-down' these energy vortices is, 'focus your awareness *onto* them, and then *away* from them'.

When you consciously 'activate' your centres, you are directing your mental awareness onto these power-points, and by a process of willpower (hence the need for a self-controlled and disciplined mind) you become more aware of the subtle vibrations of life all around you.

If, at present, you don't understand the proper function and purpose of each of your chakra-centres, or how to correctly balance the soul-energies within them, don't meddle with them.

A little knowledge can sometimes lead to danger.

Chakra-Exercise One, for Linking with your Psychic Centres

Sit in a comfortable hard-backed chair, and relax. Close your eyes and imagine or 'see' your physical body sitting on the chair, but within it visualise an exact replica, but this inner body is made up of light: it is filled with golden light. Notice how these two bodies interpenetrate each other.

Allow your inner sight to gaze at your body of light, and then visualise your seven chakras as wheels of swirling energy situated on your energy-body. See each chakra as a circling vortice of rainbow-coloured energy, about the size of a tea-saucer.

(Each energy-vortice makes a similar pattern to water as it swirls out of sight down a plug-hole in a sink.)

Working from your feet upwards: see your first chakra as a swirling vortice of energy at the base of your spine; next, see a chakra a few centimetres above your groin; next see a chakra swirling over your solar-plexus region (between your navel and the end of your breastbone); and then see a wheel of light over your heart, followed by another over your throat, and another over your third-eye centre, situated between your eyebrows and just above the bridge of your nose; and lastly, visualise a vortice of energy circling over the crown of your head. Visualise your inner body of light and all of these swirling chakras together as a composite picture; and then by an act of willpower, gently expand the rays in your body of light so that the light-energy illuminates every corner of the room.

Next, will your chakras to expand: working from the root chakra upwards, make each of them in turn become about the size of a dinner-plate.

Breathe deeply, and then relax.

Then 'return' your chakras to their normal size, and 'pull in' the rays of energy back into your body of light.

Now open your eyes and 'ground' yourself by dismissing psychic matters from your mind, and going about your daily life as usual.

Chakra-Exercise Two, for Balancing your Energy-System

Your psychic energies will fluctuate throughout your life. Sometimes you can collect a concentrated gathering of energy which can hover over certain points in your psychic system. At these times, you should try to bring your energy-system back into balance. A good time to do this chakra-balancing exercise is at night, just before you go to sleep.

Lie down on your bed, relax and calm your mind. Breathe a little more deeply than normal...then sink into deeper relaxation.

Close your eyes and try to be aware of where in your body the energy has 'gathered' or 'blocked' itself. Some people find that their solar-plexus feels 'tight' or tense; others (creative people) find that too much energy and tension has gathered around the throat chakra, which is linked to the thyroid gland; other people might experience tension or aching in their heads, at their brow or over their crown chakra.

Wherever you feel that the energy and tensions have gathered in abundance: if you're left-handed, place your right hand over that chakra-point; or if you're right-handed, place your left hand over that point, and then place your other hand at the opposite end of the chakra-system. For example, if your head energies are too strong, place one hand over your crown chakra, and the other hand over a point at the opposite end of your energy-system, either over the groin or over the root chakra.

Then, using a combination of visualisation and physical movements, sweep your flat-palmed hand and the 'gathered' energy with it towards the chakra-point that's furthest away from the 'blockage', and allow both hands to touch at the end of each movement.

Do this a few times.

Then to finish the exercise, place your main hand on top of your head and the other over your groin psychic centre, and 'will' the energies to balance themselves out, so that your psychic lights and soul-energies are equally distributed throughout your system.

Then you can go to sleep.

If you've done this exercise properly, you'll sleep as soundly as a baby and will feel much calmer and more refreshed in the morning.

5

Your Auras:
The Four Main Energy-Fields

Now let's consider another aspect of your psychic apparatus: your aura, or to be more precise, your auras.

The aura was termed by Dr Walter John Kilner 'the human atmosphere' and this is a good description, for it appears as a cloud of swirling colours surrounding all animate, and seemingly inanimate, forms. Dr Kilner was a member of the medical staff at St. Thomas's Hospital in London, and around 1908 he invented the Kilner Screen, which was made of two glass plates with a coal-tar dye (called dicyanin) placed between them.

Looking through the dye solution allowed his eyes to see into the ultra-violet band of light, and through his screen he saw misty lights around the naked bodies of his subjects. He later trained his eyes to see these energies without the use of the screen. He was looking at parts of the aura.

Then, in 1939 in Russia, Semyon Kirlian also discovered a way to photograph the strange light-emanations that surround people and objects. While watching a patient receiving treatment from a high-frequency generator, he noticed that when

51

electrodes were brought near to the patient's skin there was a small flash of light.

He and his wife followed this up by taking a picture of his own hand in the same conditions, and it was surrounded by strange light-radiations.

Scientists are still debating Kirlian's and Kilner's findings, but I believe they saw some of the lowest vibrations of the auric field, which are radiated by the physical aura.

There are several auric atmospheres.

Some esoteric schools claim there are seven main energy-fields which correspond to the seven main chakras, and to the seven planes of existence in the Spirit Realms; but these concepts remain open to question.

Your auric energies are constantly undulating and shining forth multifarious colours all around you; and contained within these energy-fields there are mental images and thought-forms, all moving around your etheric, spiritual, mental, emotional and physical bodies.

The aura is an *effect*, it is not a *cause*: it 'out-pictures' or radiates in colour the continuously-changing energies which are produced when it transforms and uses the God-force within you.

The God-Force enters through your chakras and your mind, and the aura presents a 'living picture' of this drawing-in, and then the expending, of these vital soul-energies.

Your auric fields are sensitive atmospheres or areas of receptivity and awareness, and they transmit as well as receive high-frequency psychic impressions.

If you wish to work to your maximum potential,

The Power of your Spirit

you must master the art of becoming aware of what
is happening within, or near, your own auric fields.

Does the aura vibrate?
Yes. The atoms of every life-form are in a state of
constant vibration, even when they appear to be
stationary or at rest: stones, fire, water, earth, air —
everything is made up of vibrating energy.

Through the act of existence, all energy-waves
disturb the ether around them, and your psychic
vision perceives these disturbances as sets of
undulating lights and colours.

How does the human aura originate?
Souls are Thought into existence by the Mind of
God, the Great Spirit of Consciousness, who
bestows upon their bodies, minds, and spirits the
miraculous power of life.

Through the very act of living, souls draw upon
the God-Energy that surrounds them and is within
them, and, by using it to think and move, they
transform it into waves of energy that can be seen
clairvoyantly as psychic lights and colours, which
we call the aura.

Do we have only one aura?
No, there are several auric fields (see illustration),
but the four main auras of interest to psychics,
mediums, and healers are as follows:

The Physical Aura
What does the physical aura look like?
If a person is in good health the physical aura
usually appears as a faint blue light, radiating up to

a few inches or so in depth all around the body; but there is a slight transparent gap visible between the skin and the beginning of this aura.

It was this physical aura that Dr Kilner so painstakingly observed and then catalogued in his book *The Human Atmosphere*, which was first published around 1911, and is still available today. (See *Recommended Reading*.)

When a healthy naked person is clairvoyantly examined standing against a smooth black velvet curtain, his physical aura resembles millions of feather-like strands of fine, light-blue energy, radiating outwards from his skin.

Of the four main auric fields, the physical aura is the easiest to discern because it vibrates at the lowest psychic frequency; and, of course, it is radiated by the physical body.

How does illness in the body show itself in the physical aura?
A diseased or malfunctioning organ within the body emits a lower rate of vibration than that of its healthy counterparts, and it's this lowering of frequency that manifests in the physical aura as a patch of darker light, or sometimes as a shadow, hovering over the affected region.

What happens to the physical aura when we die?
The physical aura gradually dematerialises as a dead body decays.

But the other auras will move on into the next world with the person whose consciousness has created them.

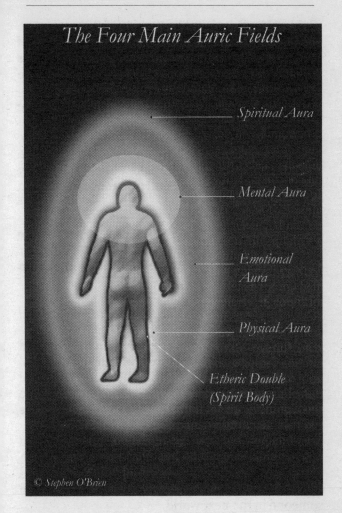

The Four Main Auric Fields

Spiritual Aura

Mental Aura

Emotional Aura

Physical Aura

Etheric Double
(Spirit Body)

© Stephen O'Brien

The Mental Aura
What does the mental aura look like?
Biblical writings describe the mental aura as a

'Golden Bowl', but, unlike the artistic halos that are depicted as crowns of light around the heads of saints, the mental aura is spherical and it radiates three-dimensionally in all directions around the head, and it also interpenetrates the body.

Its depth and shades of colour depend upon the mental and spiritual development of its creator.

Because millions of thoughts are born each day, the mental aura doesn't retain its spherical shape because thought-rays and shafts of light frequently project outwards from it, and also move inwards to penetrate it.

The more intelligence and active reasoning-power a person's mind uses, the wider is the circumference of his mental aura, and the brighter it becomes to clairvoyant vision. The mental aura is, of course, radiated by the mind.

What type of information is held in the mental auric field?
All the memories and thoughts you have ever had are either displayed or stored within your mental auric field, and these could well include facts and information about your past lives; and it's also argued by some teachers that it can contain details about your future incarnations.

It's usually the mental aura that psychics tune in to when they make a telepathic or psychic link with a client; whereas a medium tunes in to the mental aura of a spirit person when communicating with someone in the next world.

Can we block our mental aura by creating thought-forms that would act as barriers to prevent psychics from reading our personal information?

The auric fields are open to be viewed by all those who've mastered the ability. It is possible to create a fog-like cloud within your aura, but this wouldn't prevent a skilled percipient from gaining access to your thoughts.

(Incidentally: what is often presented as public mediumship is sometimes nothing more than a display of auric reading, delivered by untrained psychics who haven't yet learned the difference between working psychically and communicating with discarnate entities. More on this, later.)

The Emotional Aura

What part of man is responsible for creating the emotional aura?

The emotional aura is created by the psychic power of the mind, and it's radiated mainly by the central nervous system.

The nervous system is a highly complex and interwoven network of sensitive fibres that reach nearly every part of a physical body. Nerves are especially sensitive to feeling; however, they react not only to pain and temperature, but also to the subtle (and sometimes subconscious) thought-patterns created within the mind.

The Spiritual Aura

What kind of information is held in the spiritual aura?

The true spiritual state of your soul is indelibly impressed in your spiritual aura.

The spiritual aura contains all the knowledge and

experiences you've gained throughout your many lives – everything is recorded there: even, it's argued, details about your future incarnations.

The spiritual aura is the most difficult energy-field for clairvoyants to perceive because it's vibrating at a very high frequency.

This aura, of course, is radiated by your soul, and it encapsulates and encompasses your other auras and energy-fields, all of which mark you out as a unique and individual entity.

The Etheric Double

Does everyone, including animals, have a spirit body?

Yes: your spirit-body is your inner energy-body, or your etheric double: it's an energy-matrix that is holding the atoms of your physical body together.

When 'death' occurs and your etheric double departs with its energy-systems and auras, your physical body ceases to be 'alive' and it breaks down into the elements from which it came.

In the auric-fields illustration you can see that between the physical body and the start of the physical aura there's a thin dark gap, and this is the position of the etheric double or spirit-body and its aura.

By and large, your spirit-body is a replica of your physical body (though without any deformities or disabilities), and it's through this vehicle that you will express yourself in the eternal worlds beyond death.

*

Can I learn to see the aura?
Yes. Everyone has the potential to develop the skill of auric reading.

To see it you can use your psychic vision, or clairvoyance, but in the early stages of your development this kind of experimentation should be undertaken under the watchful eye and expert guidance of a reputable medium or tutor.

There are specific psychic exercises that can enhance your clairvoyant powers, and I'll share some of these with you later.

In mediumship, does the spirit world always work through the medium's aura?
Yes. In order for all forms of mediumship to take place, including spiritual healing and physical manifestations, the spirit helpers must blend the energies of their auric fields with those of their mediums.

If the auras of the medium, the sitters, and the spirit visitors are vibrating roughly within the same wavelengths, the thoughts of each party can be instantly received by the others.

This same process applies to psychics: they, too, work through blending their auric fields with those of their clients.

Why do some spirit guides maintain that a cheerful attitude in the medium creates 'a clear aura' through which spirit communicators may successfully transmit their thoughts?
Dark and negative thoughts vibrate at a much lower frequency than do light and happy ones. Grief, for example, often creates in the aura a

gloomy grey cloud that wraps itself around the bereaved person in an effort to protect him from intrusion at a vulnerable time. But this clouding also acts as a barrier to spirit communication being received clearly – rather in the same way as bad weather conditions impede the clear transmission and reception of radio and television signals.

But if a medium has a balanced, cheerful and outgoing personality, this generates much higher psychic vibrations, which manifest as brighter soul-lights and more vibrant energy. Optimistic thoughts act just like a battery does in a radio set: they provide extra power for signals to be received more clearly.

The same kind of psychic barriers and conditions are also encountered by spiritual healers and by psychics; but never forget that the quality of a sensitive's work will always fluctuate, for that is the nature of sensitivity, which is why each display of your abilities should be viewed as an experiment.

Can the public affect the psychic transmission and reception process?
Yes, they can.

The disinterest or boredom generated by some witnesses don't help sensitives to deliver their best work. Variety, even in the presentation of a public meeting, injects life into the psychic atmosphere and this should always be encouraged.

If the witnesses are prejudiced against the sensitive in any way, then his standard of work is nearly always of a poorer quality than normal.

*

Exercise One, for Sensing the Aura

Sit on a hard-backed chair and instruct a friend to stand a few metres behind you.

Close your eyes and ask your friend to walk silently towards you, at a time of his choosing, while you try to be aware of his presence as he approaches.

Stop him as soon as you can sense his proximity.

The further away from you he is when you detect him, the more psychically attuned to auras you are.

Exercise Two, for Sensing the Aura

Ask a colleague to sit on a hard-backed chair, then stand a few metres in front of him. Outstretch your hands so that your palms are facing your friend's body.

Close your eyes and slowly (and very carefully!) walk towards him, but stop when you can sense the 'electrical' tingling or psychic sensations of his auric field.

The further away from him when you sense his energy-field, the more sensitive to auras you are.

Exercise Three,
for Seeing the Physical Aura Clairvoyantly

This exercise works best when you have the services of a naked subject; but if you can't find anyone to co-operate (never mind!) try it this way:

Obtain some black velvet cloth and hang it (without any creases) in a corner of the room.

Dim the lights a little, and close the curtains. Relax and breathe quietly. Bare your arm (or get the subject to do so) then hold the limb directly in front of the velvet curtain.

For the next minute or two, gaze at the skin and also at the area immediately surrounding it (about a centimetre or two in depth).

Next, take your eyes slightly out-of-focus so that your vision is a little blurred. Then put your eyes back into focus, and gaze at the skin again – but don't frown or screw up your eyes; keep your vision unstrained and relaxed.

If the experiment works, you should perceive a faint smoky grey-white light all around the arm – but if you don't, keep trying!

Auric Protection

Does the aura afford any kind of protection from undesirable influences ?
Yes. A sensitive normally attracts discarnates who exist, or vibrate, at roughly the same soul-frequency as himself. If you want to benefit from the guidance of more advanced spiritual souls, you must attract them to you by developing the spiritual side of your nature.

What happens in the aura when someone sends good or bad thoughts to another person?
The transmitter of 'good' or 'bad' thoughts projects rays of energy from his mind, through his aura, towards the mind and aura of the subject.

But the receiver of this 'light' or 'dark' energy will accept it only if he wishes to. We can consciously or subconsciously reject anyone's thought-rays or their healing energies or prayers, in exactly the same way as we can refuse advice: by ignoring it, or 'blocking it out', we deny it power over us.

Advanced spirit friends, who are concerned with our spiritual progression, encourage us to send out only thoughts that are good.

Can I do any exercise to 'close down' my aura, in order to keep undesirable influences away from my sphere of sensitivity?
You can't 'close down' your aura: it's a life-energy field. You can't rip it or dent it, either.

Your aura naturally expands and contracts in line with your thoughts and feelings. An outward-looking, cheerful, positive and confident person's aura expands; conversely, a miserable, depressed or uncommunicative person's aura contracts.

Unpleasant spirit visitors make quite rare appearances, but on the occasions when someone manages to break through your natural defences, and this happens more often at night when you're drowsy and ready for sleep, there are some steps you can take:

Auric Protection, Exercise One
If you feel the presence of an undesirable entity close by, you can mentally instruct that person to go away (using any language you think will bring the desired effect), or you can contract your aura; or you can mentally wrap a cloak of light around yourself: it's all a question of visualisation and of controlling your energy-fields by an act of will.

This kind of self-defence is achieved through a psychological image-making process.

If you're in bed, get up immediately: go down-stairs and make yourself a drink, or potter around and keep busy until the atmosphere becomes calm again.

And here's a tip: from the beginning of my own work I told the spirit people, 'Bed is for sleeping.' You'd be wise to establish this precedent, and never look for spirit contact late at night.

Auric Protection, Exercise Two

You can send out an emergency call to your loved ones on the other side of life. Call them by their names, either vocally or mentally, and ask for their immediate aid to remove any intruder from the vicinity.

They will arrive within seconds, or sometimes within minutes, drawn to you by the power of your urgent thoughts.

Meanwhile, command any intruders, in language of no uncertain terms, to leave the premises immediately, spelling out the consequences if your protectors have to forcibly remove them from your presence.

Of course, you should always ask for your spirit friends' protection, as a loving mother does when she prays that her children will be kept safe by the Angel World.

Auric Protection, Exercise Three

This method is only for the naturally defensive or more aggressive types of personality: you can send out forked-lightning energies towards the intruder, like spears of light; but be aware that this action is, in fact, a form of attack and an intruder might well react and could make even more of a nuisance of himself.

Think carefully before using this method.

Colour in the Auric Fields

Why are so many sensitives at loggerheads about the meaning of the colours they perceive within the aura?
Each shade of colour in the aura has a specific meaning, but the psychic interpretations vary because so much depends on the area in which the colour occurs and on the talent and understanding of the percipient.

For example: bright yellow seen in the mental aura would indicate an active and questioning mind; but if the same colour were seen over the solar-plexus in the emotional aura, it would indicate nervousness or a highly-strung nature.

The only way to achieve a definitive interpretation of each colour in each location would be to study the recorded impressions of reputable mediums throughout the centuries, and then to correlate their findings. I've discussed colour and its interpretation more fully in my book *Angels By My Side*, but would advise any serious investigator to thoroughly research this subject and practise his skills only on emotionally-stable friends before releasing his talents upon an unsuspecting public. I'll touch upon the subject of Chromotherapy, which is healing by colour, later in this book in the section called *Everyone Can Heal: More on Unfolding your Natural Healing Powers*.

For now, see the auric colour chart on page 67.

When I'm angry, how and where does this show

itself in my aura?
Anger often shows itself as fiery red, yellow and orange flame-like lights in the emotional aura, mainly in the region over the solar-plexus, just above the navel. Of course, the mental bowl (where anger begins) also displays a mixture of these colours.

If a person is loving and compassionate, how and where would a psychic see this manifesting in the aura?
A rose-pink light would flood the emotional aura of a loving soul, mainly over the areas of the heart and the solar-plexus, but the light would also mingle its colour into other parts of the mental auric field.

Exercise for Calming your Emotions with Auric Colour

Sit comfortably and close your eyes. Visualise your aura, and within it your etheric double or spirit body. By an act of visualisation, see the ceiling above your head becoming transparent and then disappearing. Outside is the sky, and beyond this you can see the deepness of outer space. Look at the great glowing orb of the sun. Link your mind to it and allow its rays to fly through space, down through Earth's atmosphere and down through your ceiling, and then allow them to bathe your inner body of light with their golden-white regenerating energies.

Next: 'replace' the ceiling above your head.

Now that your energised aura is glowing with golden-white light, through an act of will: change the colour of this light into a pale blue radiance.

Fill your aura with a blue, peace-inducing light...

Breathe in the calmness and tranquillity of the light, as if it were made of air, until you feel more at peace with yourself. Pay particular attention to directing the pale blue light towards your third-eye, throat and solar-plexus chakras.

Breathe in the light, deeply... and then relax...

Open your eyes, then 'ground' yourself by going about your daily life as usual.

A Basic Interpretation of Colours Seen in the Mental Aura

Although the following list isn't by any means definitive, it presents general guidelines to the meaning of each bright colour when seen in the mental bowl, as a reflection of a person's character.

Red: positive
Orange: energetic
Yellow: intelligent
Green: well-adjusted
Blue: peaceful
Indigo: intuitive
Violet: spiritual
White: independent

Other Popular Colours

Black: strong
Grey: gloomy
Rose-pink: loving
Brown: earthy

6

How Spirit Communicators
use your Auric Power

*Can you tell us something about the spiritual
power contained in the aura, and how our spirit
friends use this energy to contact us?*
Yes; and I can do no better than to reproduce my
spirit guide's teachings on this important subject,
taken from my book *In Touch with Eternity,* in
which he speaks about auras, atmospheres,
spiritual and psychic powers, and how our spirit
operators use them to get in touch with us:

White Owl's Teachings:

This is how we in the spirit world perceive the
events which happen 'backstage' at public and
private séances.

Though audiences are aware of the calendar
dates and times of my medium's work, we are not
in this world, for there is no chronological (clock)
time in eternity; but I pick up Stephen's thoughts
of when a meeting is approaching.

We work with the language of Thought.

Telepathic messages are instantaneously flashed
from mind to mind in my world, and some guides
are able to transmit thoughts from one world to

another, which exists at a higher rate of vibration.

When I am aware of service to perform on Earth, after my calls to a specialised band of helpers have been transmitted, I then delegate my current activities to other people and make my way down to Mother Earth.

I home-in on the frequency of Stephen's mind (for every soul has its own unique wavelengths within which its mind vibrates).

Sometimes we find our medium driving along a motorway or just waking up in some strange hotel after having had a long conversation with me in my world while his spirit had been travelling out of the physical body, at night. Occasionally I find it necessary to remain beside my medium for the whole day on which a demonstration of psychic power is to take place, from the moment he wakes on Earth until the conclusion of our work together.

It is not my function to protect him but rather to carefully monitor his mind and emotions so that when our time of joining comes I know what has affected him on that day: how much stress, relaxation, tension, laughter, etc.

All these expended energies can help or hinder our at-one-ment, and I like to be fully informed of his activities in order that I may provide the closest possible blending of our two minds at the point of contact.

Mediums activate their own natural auric-protection; their general character and inner motivation draws unto them persons from my world who are in attunement with these forces. The only fear mediums need have of attracting any undesirable influences stems from themselves: from their own lifestyles, their own thoughts, feelings and true reasons for contact.

Now a little about the spirit power and energies we require when joining the two worlds as one, for this is an often misunderstood aspect of our work.

Everyone who attends a séance possesses an electromagnetic field of energy — an aura — which is either vibrant with electrical impulses or sometimes (more often than not) it can be rather depleted. This accounts for the differences in energy between souls who are healthy, cheerful and optimistic, and others who are depressed and miserable.

So, to us — as far as our work is concerned — each person is a unit of fluctuating energy, a battery of power, each contributing to, or drawing from, the electrical atmosphere in the auditorium and surrounding areas.

When we are confronted with a thousand miserable and depressed people then the auric power available to us is considerably diminished. This can make our task much harder because we need to blend with human electromagnetic impulses to aid our work. Black and turbulent thoughts (negative influences) impede our efforts.

What audiences contribute to public meetings is of vital importance to their success or failure. However, the medium is by far the greatest stumbling-block to our organised transmissions, as I shall soon explain.

If crowds do not emanate feelings of sympathy, kindness and attention towards Stephen then a great deal of their energies cause electrical disturbances in the auditorium, which are unhelpful, and their auric power often becomes unavailable to us.

If they are in grief, introverted, disinterested — or even bored and tired — their vital energies flow inwards, making them more difficult for us to tap.

This can drastically affect the quality of a demonstration in much the same way as a transistor radio doesn't operate properly if its batteries are low. So it is with mediumship.

Audiences create — by the blending and mixing of their auric fields — a huge photosphere of electromagnetic power (with other 'whirlpools of energy' moving within it) which is inside and often surrounding the meeting-place. When souls give their undivided attention or focus their minds on something outside of themselves, their energies flow outwards. Depending on the quality of this power our work is aided or hindered.

We sometimes convey this general power-report to our medium in his dressing-room, before he takes the platform, particularly if conditions for contact are going to be poor.

Along with his own sensitivity Stephen then obtains a reasonably accurate overall picture of audience conditions, and whether or not the people will be co-operative or reticent to join in the spontaneous three-way spirit communication link, which, of course, is vital for the evening's success.

Stephen's own expansive aura can also be full of energy or adversely depleted, depending on his physical health and on the peacefulness, or lack of it, within his mind.

When he makes contact with the public his sympathy and compassion (soul-energies) go out to them. If the people are relaxed and comfortable with him then they are particularly receptive to his power and they quickly warm to his personality.

This means that some who may have entered as cold and unresponsive beings will now — almost unconsciously — find themselves more at ease (because of interest in the medium) and hence they will automatically project and contribute more energy to the proceedings. They are now adding their personal power to his, and very often in his opening remarks we have heard Stephen say, quite correctly: 'According to what you give, so shall you receive.' This sums up the process quite well.

Without doubt, the greatest obstacle in any two-world communication is the medium.

Physical tiredness impedes our thought-flows reaching him. If the body is nervously exhausted then it cannot function properly: the body only responds clearly to mental orders when it is fit and well.

But by far the most hindering of all circumstances is the medium's mind. If a sensitive is emotionally upset or clouded by psychological concerns, this sets up swirling energy-fields which can sweep away any of our subtle thought-forces and diminish contact with us. Instead of a peaceful, calm countryside scene where silence and harmony reign and everything is in a state of equilibrium and balance — this is the ideal mind — we now have to work through a mighty cyclone which is ripping through that tranquillity; and this is the mind of a psychologically-disturbed, anxious being.

Through the generated power of our minds and auric fields — which we closely blend with Stephen's — communicators then step near to the medium and try to be heard, seen or sensed. If their attunement with his mind-frequencies is good then they are successful (usually in varying degrees). To aid this, around Stephen himself there is another sizeable group of spirit operators charging his electrical fields so that he stands within a highly sensitised sphere of energy. Communicators are then shepherded forward, one or two at a time. It is a very controlled process.

With so many varying conditions which can adversely affect our success we are always delighted when the meetings go well, for this indicates that a good job of work has been accomplished.

After all, mediums and guides have difficult tasks, delicate operations; rather like the fine tuning of a radio set to a transmitted station, the wavelength has to be just right.

We can, and do, frequently miss our channels.

7

The Difference Between Psychics and Mediums

By now you'll have realised that before dashing off to unleash your abilities on the public, there are a number of important teaching-points to consider, and here's another of these:

There's a world of difference between psychics and mediums; and there's a marked difference between psychic and mediumistic messages.

Sadly, on many public platforms today there are numerous psychics masquerading as mediums because they don't understand how their psychic apparatus is functioning, or how they can develop it correctly and use it proficiently.

Responsible sensitives must know from which sources their mental impressions and factual information originate. They should be aware that it isn't difficult to register facts psychically (i.e. telepathically) from the minds of others, from the psychic atmospheres in the séance-room, or even from the depths of their own subconscious thoughts. A proficient and progressive sensitive must learn to differentiate between the sensations that these three very different energy-vibrations can generate in the mind.

If you've not yet mastered this skill, then you're in danger of deluding yourself into thinking you're a medium, when in fact you might only be a psychic – that is: someone who works as a telepath who links only to earthly minds, or to impressions that remain close to the physical world.

How, then, can you tell if you're a psychic or a medium?

Well, there are several important indicators, and here are the main ones:

If you persist in selecting the recipients of your messages from a crowd people, it's quite possible that you might become caught in a 'psychic trap', because whenever *you* choose your recipients the spirit world must stand silently beside you, for you disempower them. Here's the golden rule:

A psychic directs his own work, but a medium's work is directed by spirit-world inspirers.

A psychic selects a recipient in a crowd and then gives that person a message simply because that person has caught his attention.

For example, a woman sitting in an audience might have a friendly smile, or might be wearing bright and cheerful clothing, and the psychic may simply feel drawn to her. There could be several reasons to account for this kind of attraction: the woman could be telepathically willing the psychic to speak to her; or, desperate to receive any kind of guidance, she might unknowingly generate and then direct towards the sensitive an invisible beam of energy that might catch his attention.

Perhaps the woman's soul is vibrating on roughly the same frequency as that of the psychic, who therefore finds it easy to link telepathically with her. Or the psychic might become aware that she's in pain, or that she's grieving, and his compassion (or his determination to succeed) might persuade him to forge a telepathic link with her.

When making such direct mind-to-mind energy-links with members of the public, a psychic's senses will automatically scan their auric atmospheres. This explains why some psychics also see thought-forms hovering in the energy-fields of the people sitting next to their recipients; and then they glimpse another image in the mind of the audience member sitting next in line, or in the seat behind – and so on, *ad infinitum*.

But none of these skills makes the exponent a medium because psychics personally direct their work, whereas a medium's work is largely directed by invisible intelligences in the world of spirit.

To avoid working psychically, and to firmly establish that you're working only mediumistically, learn to disregard any feelings or thoughts you receive from your sitters; and, instead, listen more attentively to your spirit communicators.

Here are the key points to remember:

- *Psychics direct their attention to the people on Earth, but mediums must direct their attention to the people in the Spirit World.*

- *In your early years of mediumistic development, don't select the recipients of your messages: link up only with your spirit-world communicators, who must first provide you with precise information to identify themselves, then they alone should direct you to speak to the correct recipient.*

These skills are difficult to achieve because they rely solely upon the medium's ability to tune-in to the minds of discarnate intelligences, but after a long period of disciplined and diligent practice your mediumship will eventually strengthen and will become more reliable.

Could anyone develop the power to make psychic links with the minds of others?
Yes, but aspirants should remember that they will achieve varying degrees of success.

Do we receive psychic impressions daily, whether we know it or not?
Broadly speaking, yes. Psychic links are registered along a mind-to-mind or soul-to-soul connection; each of us daily forges these subtle contacts either consciously or subconsciously.

Do you agree that psychics can perceive only the thoughts that are currently in their sitters' minds?
No, I don't. A well developed psychic can perceive thoughts buried in the deepest regions of a sitters' subconscious mind.

Notable researchers and respected mediums have conducted countless telepathic experiments and have proved this beyond doubt. Psychics can glean precise family names, addresses, powerful desires, past hopes, and traumatic events that have happened to you etc.

I heard of one case in which a so-called medium described to his sitter a very flamboyant spirit communicator who was wearing a full Cavalier outfit, complete with ostrich feather plumes, a gleaming sword and buckled boots.

But the sitter replied, 'That's interesting. You've just described the principal character in the novel I'm writing.' On this occasion, the medium was merely a psychic who had registered the thought-form of a fictional character in his sitter's mind.

This is a thought-provoking lesson, upon which all sensitives would be wise to contemplate.

During one of your teaching seminars you informed a student medium she was giving out psychic messages and not mediumistic ones. What exactly did you mean?

If the medium was working psychically, I meant she was obtaining factual information by directing the beam of her awareness toward the minds of her sitters and then she was reading their thoughts and auras, instead of getting into contact with the spirit communicators who were gathered around her on the platform.

I shall repeat again this important teaching-point: both psychic and mediumistic messages rely upon a telepathic contact being made, but psychics link with the minds of people living on the Earth, whereas mediums contact the minds of discarnate people.

It's all a question of discipline: exponents must learn to mentally direct and control their energies. Mediums, especially, must learn to give their full attention to the spirit people, and not to tap into the thoughts of their recipients.

Is flower-clairsentience a mediumistic skill?
No; flower clairsentience (which means flower clear-sensing) is a purely psychic ability which has nothing to do with contacting discarnate intelligences. It's a form of **psychometry**: *Psyche* is a Greek word meaning Soul and *Metron* means to measure – a good translation of this is 'a measure of the soul of things'.

Some clairsentients start with a psychic or telepathic reading of their sitter's energy-vibrations, which have been impressed upon the auric fields surrounding the flower, and then they try to receive mediumistic contacts from the spirit world for that person: but this leads to confusion because mediumship and psychic work are two separate and distinct skills.

Why do I sometimes hear spirit voices when I'm using my psychic powers to read the tarot cards for my clients?
You obviously possess mediumistic potential, and with the right kind of training you could develop this further. Meanwhile, discipline yourself to use one skill or the other.

I get precognitive dreams: are these reaching me from spirit communicators or are they psychic impressions?
You don't need the help of discarnate entities to glean your own future, or to dream of the sets of possibilities that might await others.

During sleep, when your spirit is freed from your body, your mind can scan the Time-stream, so to speak – if you've developed this skill, of course.

Sometimes, however, you might receive these precognitive images from your spirit friends.

I was told by a medium that I'd been a tyrannical Pharaoh in a previous life. Was this a psychic message?
It's anybody's guess!

But it's possible that the sensitive gleaned this information from your Higher Self, or he might have registered a secret fear or desire within your subconscious mind.

Thoughts are living things.

8

Spirit Guides, and Spirit Controls

Whichever branch of soul-awareness you practise, you now know that you will attract to yourself the influence of discarnate minds. Here are some of the more important points to remember about these personalities who might try to help you with your work.

What is a spirit guide?
A spirit guide is a discarnate personality who has attached him- or herself to someone destined to become a medium for the world of spirit.

How do I get a spirit guide?
Once you embark upon the path of unfolding your soul-sensitivity, your thoughts and desires radiate from your mind and into the next world and the spirit people register them, because your mind is open to them, and a guide will be forthcoming.

Who are our spirit guides and our spirit controls?
They are quite fallible discarnate personalities whose self-appointed task is that of trying to communicate with the Earthworld.

They should never be treated as gods or as the

founts of all wisdom. If anyone in the next world demands your co-operation or seeks to dominate your will, then recognise you've drawn to yourself a quite unevolved inspirer. In such a case, you should immediately put your mind and character in order before continuing your unfoldment.

Are my guides members of my own family who have preceded me into the next world?
Sometimes they are, but more often than not they're individuals who, through the law of soul-attraction, have been drawn close to the Earth to help you to unfold and train your soul-awareness.

How can I discover the identity of my guide?
This information will be given to you only if your guide thinks it necessary. A great number of spirit helpers work quietly in the background and feel disinclined to identify themselves.

It's better to forget about your guides' names and, instead, judge them by the quality of the work they do.

Why are many guides Native American Indians, Chinese Mandarins, or African Zulus?
Spirit friends and helpers come from all walks of life, from many countries and from different times in history. It's a generally-held misconception that many guides originate from the above-mentioned races.

The following text is reproduced from my book *Angels By My Side*, from the chapter in which my own spirit guide is questioned on guardian angels and spirit controls. The questions to him are printed in *italics*:

I would like to know who guides me.
I must tell you: it is very easy for me to clearly read that thought from your mental aura. Let me now explain what could happen if you keep this idea in your mind.

Through the Laws of Attraction, you will draw to you someone from my world who would like to work with you, but they may be hindered by this dominant guide-thought in your mentality.

Your spirit friend will want to get on with the important work, while your dominating desire will be to know your guide's identity.

Furthermore, if you wish for a certain type of guide, a colourful personality — such as one of those you have already mentioned — then the intelligence working with you will be obliged to meet that powerful desire-force, in order for the lines of communication to be opened up, so that the work may progress.

You mean they would lie to me?
No, they would meet your need: it is you who would lie to yourself.

We are not interested in names, positions or high-sounding titles, we are concerned with helping the Great Spirit's Truths to liberate man's mind from ignorance and fear.

But your remarks indicate that mediums may mislead people.
Mediums are only human beings, my friend, and quite fallible ones at that. They, like we who are in Spirit, will doubtless make many silly mistakes.

As far as Our Side is concerned, communication is not as easy as it might sometimes appear. We try to blend our minds and personalities with those of our mediums and we are not always as successful as we would like to be, owing to mental, spiritual, emotional and physical conditions obstructing our efforts at the time of contact.

So, are some guides purely thought-forms, or thought-images that have been created by the minds of their mediums?
Yes, some are just that.

Thought-forms of (let us say) an elderly Chinese mandarin would appear just like pictures hovering within the mind of the sensitive who has formed them, created by his desire-force because he wants this kind of person to make contact with him.

These images have no real life of their own but they can be seen by us, and sometimes psychically aware people on Earth are talented enough to attune their perceptive powers into the mental frequencies of the medium and to clearly register these thought-forms–

– Through telepathy?
– yes; and then the psychic describes this thought-image to its own creator, to the sensitive.

The medium then goes home believing he has an old Chinaman as his guide, which is exactly what he thought he had, and what he wanted to hear, is it not?

Yes. But genuine guides do exist?
Oh yes; I am one of them.

*

86

Stephen, what are the responsibilities of a spirit guide?
A medium's spirit guide is an old friend or a soul-partner, a spiritual advisor who's interested in the growth of his medium's character and personality, and in the unfoldment of his spiritual work. Many guides claim to be part of a greater hierarchy in the realms of spirit, and that they've been imbued with a spiritual mission which they're trying to fulfil through their mediums.

Can one spirit guide inspire and influence two different mediums?
Yes, if he wishes; though it's more usual for a spirit guide to build up a close association with only one medium.

Will my guide or my 'Doorkeeper' protect me from 'evil' influences?
Sensitives can sometimes be aware of all manner of personalities in the Beyond, but they can also be surrounded and supported by beloved discarnate friends, especially at times of service or spiritual need.

Fear is born of ignorance, and whenever this question of protection arises you should examine your reasons for posing it, for you might discover a fear within you which should be eradicated and replaced by knowledge.

'Doorkeepers' are just spirit people working in your team, and they help to keep you safe from disturbing influences close to the séance-room. Try not to get weighed down by terms and titles.

What is a spirit control?
A spirit control is a discarnate person who's mastered, or is learning to master, the skill of mind-to-mind communication with a medium on the Earth.

What are the responsibilities of a spirit control?
When a séance or a meeting is to take place the spirit control closely attunes himself to his medium's mind and acts as a kind of mental 'bridge' across which communication between the two worlds can take place.

How are spirit controls trained to work with their mediums?
The worlds of spirit are highly organised. They have colleges that specialise in training discarnates to become spirit controls or guides, in which all the complex processes of mental communication are studied and practised.

When mediums' bodies are asleep at night, and their etheric doubles are in the astral worlds (those planes of thought nearest to the Earth) they practise the art of telepathic communication with their spirit controls.

Practice makes perfect.

Will my spirit control always work with me?
There's usually a succession of different controls working with a medium, and as the medium progresses and becomes more sensitive to the spirit world's vibrations, he earns for himself the guidance of more advanced controls.

Some mediums, however, seem to associate with

the same set of helpers right throughout their years of service.

How does the guide or control get into contact with his medium?
The guide usually has to think himself back towards the Earthplane and then, through his power of thought, he homes-in on the unique vibration of his medium's mind, and arrives in the séance-room.

It isn't essential for the guide to stand beside his medium when working, though this method is preferred. On Earth, radio sets can be miles from a radio mast but they'll still receive the signals if the conditions are favourable; this same principle applies to mediumship.

In order for any mediumship to operate (and this includes spiritual healing) mental attunement must take place. If the guide's thought-patterns can closely approximate those of his medium, the lines of communication are established.

How can I help my guide to get a better mental link with me?
Learn to calm your mind, and quieten it of any turbulent or negative thoughts. Expect success. Be optimistic and cheerful. Never panic; never doubt or fear, for these conditions act as barriers to receiving clear communications from the next world.

Our spirit friends' thoughts vibrate at much higher frequencies than our own, and the slightest psychological disturbance in a medium's mind can sweep away their subtle contacts. Master these mental skills and your guide will be able to more closely attune with you, and your mediumship will operate more effectively.

When presenting survival evidence, do mediums work with their spirit controls or directly with spirit communicators?
In the earlier stages of development it's usual for a medium to work closely with one control whom he's chosen in his sleep-life, until his sensitivity is firmly established.

After mediums have gained considerable work experience, the controls tend to step back to allow their mediums to link directly with the minds of spirit communicators.

But to take this important step too soon can result in the developing medium becoming quite confused, because the average spirit visitor hasn't mastered the art of communicating his thoughts coherently.

My control is from a foreign nation, but why do I 'hear' him speaking in English?
The true language of the spirit is Thought, and this can be communicated without the need for speech.

When your spirit receives another person's thoughts, your mental faculties transform these into symbols or words that you can understand.

Language is a human invention: but Thought has no language.

However, on the Other Side there are also interpreters working with the spirit people who wish to communicate in their own tongue, and their messages can be translated and then given to the medium in his own language.

Interestingly enough, some guides maintain they had to master their mediums' Earth languages before they could work together successfully.

Why doesn't my control give me detailed facts to prove survival to the public in a more convincing way?
Spiritual guides are not concerned with satisfying their mediums' egos: their objective is to touch the souls and minds of humankind, and to make us think more deeply about spiritual issues.

When sitting quietly in silence, a medium can discuss with his helpers the way in which he'd like to see his mediumship progressing, and even if he receives no answers or guiding comments, his thoughts will be noted.

But when service is being rendered, a medium can give only what he's able to receive – and the messages are usually carefully prepared by the communicators and spirit controls to meet the needs of the recipients.

Why hasn't my guide developed my inner senses of seeing, hearing and sensing (clairvoyance, clairaudience, and clairsentience) to a much greater pitch?
The unfolding of your psychic awareness is your responsibility, and not your guide's.

Mediums must develop their own soul sensitivity, usually through sitting in the silence and learning to quieten their minds so that they may more clearly perceive the subtle thought-flows that are being transmitted to them by spirit beings.

First and foremost, all aspiring mediums must learn to discipline their thoughts, and then it would benefit them to undertake a programme of psychic exercises (preferably under the supervision of an experienced tutor) to awaken and strengthen their psychic abilities.

It is the mediums who limit the spirit world's ability to operate successfully in this world.

I'm a medium, but sometimes when I'm about to work I get frightened because I can't sense my spirit friends standing next to me. Your opinions on this would be helpful.
Never be afraid.

Fear clouds your thought processes and makes it much more difficult for you to receive clear communication. Your spirit friends will certainly be with you because they're aware of your thoughts about the service, long before you arrive at the meeting-place.

Place your trust in your guides and helpers and, whether you sense them near to you or not, know that they are there.

When I've given what I term 'a poor service' – that is, a demonstration of mediumship which doesn't contain enough evidence of survival – why has this happened?
Either your psychic sensitivity hasn't unfolded to the point where you can clearly see, hear, and sense your communicators, or your mental attunement with your spirit friends hasn't been correctly established.

A poor state of attunement is usually the cause of

'a poor service'; nevertheless, the meeting may have contained important spiritual lessons for all those who experienced it, don't you think?

At this stage in your journey, you've become acquainted with several psychic and spiritual laws and you should also have thought seriously about your motivation. If you've completed this ground-work, and you're still intent on developing your psychic, mediumistic or healing powers, you're ready to sit for their unfoldment.

9

Running a Successful Psychic Circle

Whether you wish to develop psychic skills, mediumistic abilities, or spiritual healing powers, I'd advise you to sit in a circle for development.

This chapter outlines some of the universally accepted guidelines for forming, running, and benefiting from attending a well-run circle; and as you'll see, if you can't find a good group to join, you can start your own.

What is a psychic awareness circle?
A psychic awareness circle is composed of a group of dedicated and earnest people seeking spiritual truth; they sit together, usually for one evening per week, to discover and then develop their innate soul-sensitivities.

How many people should there be in a home-circle or in a spiritual awareness class?
I would recommend at least two (!) but about eight to ten people can be trained comfortably.

Should sitters choose their seats according to their gender and because of the degree of psychic power they possess?

It's said that the Nazarene, who is referred to by some teachers as one of the greatest spiritual mediums, was supported by twelve psychically gifted men, which seems to nullify the theory that sitters should be placed in a circular male/female (positive/negative) energy formation.

But I think it's sensible for sitters to keep their positions in the group, once they've been firmly established.

Who should choose the leader of a circle: the inspirers in the Beyond, or the group's members?
A natural selection process will operate, but the leader should be the person who has the greatest spiritual and psychic knowledge with which he can guide the class, or the most practical experience of mediumship, through which the spirit world may inspire the group.

What's the most important factor needed to make any circle successful?
The presence of love and harmony between all the sitters is essential for the success of any circle.

When minds and souls are vibrating in harmony, and when sitters are friendly and understanding toward one another, the energy of love flows freely around the group – and this is the greatest power of all.

Should a circle's members all sit to develop one medium, psychic or healer in the group, or should each person aim for individual unfoldment?
As a general rule, and particularly if the circle is newly formed, it's wise to sit as a happy group of

friends in which each person seeks individual unfoldment.

However, some groups are directed by their spirit guides to contribute their psychic and spiritual energies toward the development of a specific medium among them, who might possess outstanding potential.

Always follow the sensible instructions from your spirit guides and inspirers, but never relinquish your right to question them.

How can I judge if the circle I attend is being conducted correctly?
Dedicated persons should meet regularly once or sometimes twice weekly, keeping to the same days and the same set times. Start and finish the circle within a three-hour period; and remember that no one in the spirit world is at your beck-and-call.

Punctuality, Patience and Perseverance will be needed, because satisfactory results are often slow to make an appearance.

Once you've started sitting as a group, the gathering should be closed to new members. There are exceptions to this rule, of course, (as there are to any rules) but remember that new entrants can often put back the group's progression because of their ignorance of spiritual matters, and because of the influence of their invisible friends, as well as their unfamiliar psychic energies.

About eight sitters is sensible number to start a new group, and if it consists of four men and four women, so much the better, for males and females generate different positive and negative psychic influences in the gathering. But ultimately, gender is unimportant; what really matters in the group is:

- **Harmony** between all the personalities.
- **Dedication** and **Commitment** from each member.
- **Sincere Motivation** from all the seekers who should be searching to attain truth, light, knowledge, guidance and inspiration from the most evolved spirit sources available. Sitters should be thoughtful and compassionate.
- **Humility**: there's an art to being a student.
- **Discipline**: mental discipline is essential if a group is to progress in an orderly fashion.
- **Obedience**: not a blind but a questioning obedience; and a gracious acknowledgement of the circle leader's experience and authority to direct the group.
- **A Thirst for Knowledge and a Desire to Progress:** the best sitters seek to build their wisdom and increase their intellectual capacity.

Remember that into the gathering each member brings his or her own general mind-frequency; so, take great care when selecting your sitters. Look into a man's heart and try to perceive his true character and his true state of spiritual evolution before inviting him to share in the power of the spirit with you. Your circle leader should possess sufficient soul-awareness to undertake this task.

What Kind of Circle Do you Want?

What is the objective of your Circle? What is your group trying to achieve?

There are many kinds of groups: there are circles for developing your Psychic-Awareness or Soul-

Sensitivity; there are Healing circles, Physical Mediumship circles, circles purely for Psychic Development; Trance circles; circles to encourage Inspirational Speaking, and so on. Which one of these avenues (or any other of the many pathways) have you a mind to pursue?

After your group members have sat together for about six months, they should have a serious discussion about the direction they'd like to take. At this time: listen to the thoughts and feelings of all the members, *on both sides of the veil.*

Pay particular attention to what your spirit helpers have to say on this important matter, for, after all, they can see the group's potential much more clearly than you can.

If your circle knows where it is now, and then it decides on where it would like to be in a year's time – it immediately has a clear direction to take.

'Rescue' Circles

I shall now tread on a number of toes.

Some people set up what are known as Rescue circles, in which mediums sit to 'rescue' lost and wandering souls in the spirit world.

Let me state categorically: *there are no lost souls in the world of spirit.*

Every soul is known; each soul is accounted for. The only way in which a soul can feel lost is in the emotional or psychological sense, much as people on Earth can feel lost when they lose sight of their purpose or their zest for life.

But in truth, no one is lost: confused, maybe; labouring under delusions of grandeur, perhaps; or 'mentally trapped' or 'emotionally crippled' by religious or moral beliefs – but certainly not lost.

If you intend to get involved with Rescue circles, exercise caution. I'm not alone in having witnessed some ridiculous posturing and ranting performed and dramatised by so-called 'trance mediums' in these circles. I recall one occasion when a group rescued a spirit fisherman who'd been struck down by lightning in the 1700s. They claimed the poor soul needed counselling and convincing that he was dead, because he was still trying to land a large fish.

After three hundred years?

I don't think so.

If anyone learns anything at all from reading this book it surely must be this: *use your intelligence.*

Always use common sense when investigating any paranormal activity.

Even in this Earthworld when a person's reported missing, someone, somewhere knows where that soul is: don't forget there are many invisible spirit friends attached to each one of us, and they are neither blind nor deaf.

Furthermore, if lost entities are brought into a Rescue circle to speak through a trance-medium, who brought them there?

Some of these souls claim they wandered into the light, and when they speak through the medium the circle members counsel them.

Here, I strongly emphasise that there are very real dangers involved in giving any type of counselling or advice to any soul, in any world, at any time, particularly if you're not a qualified practitioner. Counselling should be given only by professionally trained people.

Amateur psychologists can severely damage the often fragile and unstable mentalities of their patients – so don't counsel unless you've been trained.

I'll be discussing this topic more fully, later in the book.

Our rescue medium claims that suicides, and morally-corrupt people, such as tyrants and despots, are suffering in an outer darkness in the spirit world. What are you thoughts on this?
All souls dwell in the light.

It's true that some of the darker and more troubled mentalities inhabit worlds in the spirit realms that are darker in appearance than the brighter and more luminous worlds of love and light, but these souls are not outcast or 'burning in the fires of Hell'. That is theological nonsense.

Heaven and Hell aren't geographical locations, they're purely states of mind. We create our surroundings in the spirit spheres by the power of and quality of our thoughts, just as we do here on Earth.

Progression is open to every soul.

Help is available to any troubled soul, in any world, provided that they ask for it.

These distraught souls need our prayers and the loving ministrations of the spirit people.

But in our rescue circle we've helped many lost souls; though if, as you claim, there are no such things as lost souls, what then is our medium doing when she contacts them and they're in great distress when they control her, and we have

to talk some sense into them?
What indeed? You tell me.

Surely, it's obvious that the spirit people are much nearer to these so-called 'lost souls' than your medium friend is?

Perhaps someone ought to explain this to her.

*

Why do you advocate that sensitives should be trained how to use their natural psychic abilities?
The best way to learn how to master your psychic and mediumistic abilities is to be carefully guided and instructed by a genuine tried-and-tested medium or psychic exponent who's walked this path before you, by someone who's experienced its depths as well as its heights, and who's encountered its benefits as well as some of the dangers and pitfalls that can occur along it.

Reputable mediums and disciplined healers and psychics can offer their students a priceless wealth of knowledge, advice, and sensible guidance.

I can't find a local circle to join. Although I'm not an experienced medium, healer or psychic, would it be safe to start a group of my own?
Yes, but do try your best to engage the services of a reputable medium or a psychically gifted teacher because your new group would benefit from being led by someone who can see the spirit people and listen to their guidance.

I run a private home-circle: how should I choose new sitters for it?

When assessing potential sitters, a circle leader's first consideration should be to uncover each aspirant's true reasons for wanting to develop his soul powers.

Psychic potential should always take second place to the importance of spiritual motivation.

Is it necessary to open and close our circles with a prayer?

No, but I would advise it because the act of prayer generates a more spiritual frame of mind in the sitters, and this will encourage them to lift their thoughts up and away from earthly things and towards their Creator, towards the source of all power. In paying homage to God, we strike a note of humility in our souls.

But with or without prayer, the circle will attract to itself the spiritual counterparts of its members.

If the members desire the guidance of wise and spiritually advanced souls, they must increase their knowledge of spiritual matters and try to attain a measure of the wisdom they seek to attract.

All aspirants should read widely, study carefully, and think seriously about as many spiritual truths and teachings as possible.

Ignorance and mental laziness should always be discouraged; and the introduction of a question-and-answer session, or a weekly philosophical discussion is recommended.

But remember it is your motivating thoughts that will draw your spiritual counterparts into the circle.

Will our spirit guides protect our circle?

Yes. Your spirit operators will do their best to repel from the séance-room any undesirable influences; nevertheless, and for obvious reasons, you should be very particular about with whom you sit to unfold and extend your soul-sensitivity.

Can circles be influenced by mischievous entities, also known as Earthbound spirits?
Yes they can, but only when the sitters, themselves, provide access to these influences.

Many circles are composed of intelligent and compassionate folk who are attended by helpers of a similar nature and motivation. This law applies to any gathering of souls. Lawyers attract legal minds; racists attract hateful spirits; and healers attract spiritual mentalities etc.

The universal laws operate unfailingly in the case of any group.

If the sitters aren't spiritually motivated to serve mankind, it's relatively easy for them to receive the spurious guidance of ignorant and self-centred souls whose materialistic thoughts still bind them close to the Earth.

If you suspect you've joined such a circle, leave it immediately; unless, of course, you intend to stay to educate its sitters.

Each week our leader makes us sing continuously for over forty minutes 'to raise the psychic-energy vibrations'. Is this productive; and what does 'raising the vibrations' mean?
I admire your stamina!

Music, like everything else in existence, is made up of energy-vibrations; and singing, of course, brings all the sitters' minds together in one harmonious accord.

Voices raised in unison can help to heighten and sensitise the psychic atmosphere in the séance-room because they provide our spirit guides with extra sound-energy vibrations.

But all things should be taken in moderation. Why not play some tapes, CDs, or records, to which you can sing along whenever necessary?

For several months I've felt uncomfortable with my circle leader's personality; to me, she seems rather bossy and lacking in compassion. Should I leave the group?

If I were you I'd discuss the matter privately with her to see if a mutual understanding can be reached. If this fails, I'd leave the circle and find a new group in which I felt more in harmony with its leader and members.

Remember: in all awareness groups, including spiritual healing and physical mediumship circles, the more spiritual the sitters' minds are, the better the results will be.

There's a lot of acrimony in the awareness class I take, which I feel I can't resolve. Have you any advice for me?

If the members of any group cannot graciously accept their differences, then the group should be disbanded. Petty jealousies and bitter thoughts are disruptive, negative forces that shouldn't be present in a properly conducted group. A wise medium described such an unsettling influence thus: 'One rotten apple got into the barrel, and it turned the rest sour.'

I've sat in mediumship awareness circles for twenty-two years, and I still can't see, sense, or hear the spirit world: why is this?
You've obviously not created within yourself the right psychic conditions for spirit communication to take place.

Many circles encourage their members to relax their bodies but fail to teach them how to master the art of quietening their thoughts, which is the keystone upon which all successful mediumship, psychic work, and spiritual healing power is built.

The simple act of attending your circle each week will not, in itself, develop your innate sensitivity; you should humbly offer yourself in service to God, to the world of spirit, and to the service of human-kind, but make certain you're in the right frame of mind when you sit.

You'll need plenty of patience and should be prepared to wait for the burgeoning of your natural soul-sensitivity – it cannot, and should not, ever be forced.

In the case of two-world communication, there is no such thing as instant mediumship – it has to be earned; and this, as in all other areas of soul progression, is usually a gradual process.

Should we sit in darkness or in red light to develop mental mediumship; that is: the abilities of clairvoyance, clairaudience, or clairsentience?
For the development of mental mediumship, neither darkness nor red light is necessary, but a subdued, soft light certainly helps to relax the

sitters' eyes and it can also create a calm ambience in the room.

Red light, which has the lowest frequency light-energy-waves in the visible spectrum, is usually employed when developing physical manifestations such as the materialisation of spirit persons, because ectoplasm (the substance which spirit operators withdraw from the medium and the sitters in order to build up their temporary physical forms) often reacts unfavourably to strong rays of white light.

But once the phenomena is well established (and this could take years of dedicated sitting) the materialised forms of spirit people often walk around the room in good red light.

However, materialisations in bright sunlight and in moonlight have also been witnessed, though these kinds of manifestations are rare indeed.

Why, in physical mediumship circles, which claim to have produced phenomena in the dark, do some spirit guides refuse to allow infra-red video cameras into the séance-room? Surely these cameras would verify the genuineness of the phenomena?

If a group can set up in the séance-room infra-red cameras or binoculars that emit no strong white-light rays, but which can convert pitch-darkness into virtual daylight, I can see no reason why any genuine spirit guide would refuse permission to use this equipment.

Some Do's and Don'ts
When Sitting in a Development Class

Sensitives must possess disciplined minds: your mind is the tool of your vocation, and you must bring it under your control. To help you in your efforts to establish more mental discipline, study the following list of basic Do's and Don'ts, the reasons for which are self-explanatory.

When sitting in your circle:

- Do remember that you're only just beginning.
- Do follow the sensible advice and direction given by your circle leader.
- Do obey your circle leader, who, in turn, should be obeying the guidance of higher intelligences who are trying to help the circle.
- Do be relaxed in body; and do remain silent.
- Do maintain a sense of harmony, both within yourself and within the group.
- Do remember that all psychic and spiritual experiences are registered by your mind, and not by your body.
- Do raise your thoughts and try to reach your highest aspirations.
- Do instil a sense of tranquillity within your mind.
- Do keep mentally alert, and try to be aware of the images and feelings that may present themselves on 'the mirror of your mind'.
- Do be cheerful, optimistic and happy while you're 'tuned-in'.
- Do be loving, kind and sympathetic to your friends in both worlds.

- Do anticipate any spirit contact or psychic manifestation with joy and gratitude.
- Do be patient, and remain humble.
- Do 'Wait upon the Messengers', and then welcome them when they arrive.
- Do listen, look, and sense, and be aware of any presences near to you.
- Do remember the guidance, inspirational thoughts, and clairvoyant messages that you might receive in your quiet time.
- Do analyse everything you're taught, no matter who teaches it to you.
- Do exert mental and emotional discipline; and exercise self-control at all times.
- Do remember that the information you receive may not always be clearly transmitted or always be correct: the spirit people, just like us, are quite fallible and they make plenty of mistakes. Communications can be serious, frivolous, or instructive.

- Don't break the silence.
- Don't try to blank your mind; this is an impossible task – simply try to quieten it.
- Don't make unreasonable demands on the spirit people or on the circle leader.
- Don't delude yourself into thinking you're a special superhuman being: you are not.
- Don't forget: you are a disciple, you're not a sergeant major.
- Don't harbour bitter, aggressive, or jealous thoughts or feelings towards anyone in the group.
- Don't create mental disharmony within yourself, or within the circle.

- Don't allow your ego to make a fool of you by grimacing, performing, or trying to be clever etc.
- Don't be unkind to the spirit people, or to your fellow sitters.
- Don't forget that your thoughts are real, and that your inspirers can see them.
- Don't enter into guide-worship; your controls are ordinary human beings, not gods.
- Don't fall asleep: you're in an awareness class!
- Don't encourage yourself to fall into power-draining trance states.
- Don't forget to tune-out just before the circle ends, and then return to full normality.
- Don't forget to say 'thank you' to all of your friends and co-operators in both worlds.

Picking up on one of the above points, you should avoid like the plague any foolish, unintelligent, degrading, reason-insulting or eccentric behaviour that marks out a circle as being the weekly sport of unenlightened Earthbound inspirers from the next world.

And, for obvious reasons, you shouldn't sit alone for mediumistic development: whenever possible, place yourself in the hands of intelligent and experienced tutors, and I mean people living on Earth and not in the next world.

10

Entering the Silence

No matter how you decide to use your sensitivity, daily periods of silence should be incorporated into your life.

Is absolute silence a necessary ingredient in all kinds of awareness and development groups?
Yes.

On circle nights, some groups play ambient background music, and if this helps to instil a sense of calmness in their physical bodies and mental fields, all well and good, but it's preferable to sit in absolute and unbroken silence for at least half an hour, which should extend to one hour once the circle is firmly established.

During this quiet time, members learn how to discipline their minds, how to relax their bodies, and how to still all turbulent and anxious thoughts.

Once they've attained a state of tranquillity, the members are more likely to register the fine, subtle wavelengths of thought that are being radiated by their guiding intelligences.

During the silence: release the tension in your body and then try to quieten your chattering mind. Enter the silence and swim in its velvet embrace, and you'll soon discover that silence is actually full of sound, both in the physical and especially in the esoteric (or inner) sense. In no circumstances whatsoever should this silence be broken – not by incarnates or by discarnates – harmony and discipline should be strictly upheld.

Anyone who breaks the silence might disturb the delicate thought-patterns of his fellows. There'll be plenty of time to speak, later on.

Visualisation and Meditation

In the early stages of development circles, some leaders (all of whom should remain aware of everything that happens in the gathering) employ the art of creative visualisation.

They gently talk to their deeply relaxed students and then take them on mental journeys into the realms of imagery, thoughts and feelings; and these mind-journeys provide invaluable experience because they take place in an inner world to which all aspirants must accustom themselves – the spirit realms are thought-planes.

Could you suggest any visualisation exercises that might help us to discipline our mental processes when we're sitting in our circle?
Yes, I can.

Visualisation Exercise One
The circle leader quietens the group, and they all close their eyes.

Some relaxing, ambient music is played while the leader describes some vivid countryside scenes. In

112

this creative visualisation exercise, the group takes a mind-journey into the vivid sights, sounds and feelings of a spirit summer countryside scene.

The leader addresses the whole group but speaks as if talking to a single individual, giving gentle commands and suggestions such as, 'You now find yourself standing beside a fast-flowing mountain stream, and in the distance you can see a crystal-clear waterfall (*seeing*). Walk up to the waterfall and place your hands inside the cascading water, and feel its coolness running over your skin (*feeling*); and listen to the birds singing joyously in the high trees all around you (*hearing*).

And so on...

During pleasant mind journeys like this one, in which the group experiences a kind of 'building castles in the air' daydream state, the sitters can be transported to any time and place that the mind can imagine.

The object of these visualisation exercises is to make the students more aware of what they can mentally see, sense, and hear with their inner soul-senses. Eventually, this will help them to become more aware of their thoughts.

(Circle leaders: I've recorded a number of these mind-journey meditations, which may assist your group. Details are at the back of this book, and the titles to look for are: 4 Meditations *and* 4 Visualisations.*)*

Visualisation Exercise Two

The circle leader takes the group on a mind journey to experience the sights and sounds of the seaside.

'Feel the sand between your toes (*feeling*); listen to the seagulls squawking, and watch them as they fly high above the mountainous cliffs (*hearing and seeing*). Sense the joy of Mother Nature all around you (*sensing*). Now stoop down and pick up from the golden sands a large seashell and place it over your ear: listen to the sound of the waves in it, (*hearing*) and then try to hear the quiet mind-voice contained within the wave-sound.

'The voice will give you a message about...(*choose one or more of the following topics*)... and you will remember the words you receive':

+ It might reveal a part of your destiny.
+ It might reveal your spirit guide's identity.
+ It might speak about the development of your spirituality or your soul-sensitivity.
+ It might suggest where some improvements can be made to your character or personality.
+ It may offer a possible solution to a difficult problem.
+ It might deliver a warning statement.
+ It might deliver a philosophical discourse, etc.

Afterwards, the class members can discuss their experiences during refreshments.

Caution: *When interpreting messages, the leader should be aware that the 'voice' usually belongs to the student's own subconscious mind, which may speak about his hopes, fears, or a possible solution to current difficulties. Just as in dreams, the symbols can be fully understood only by the student, and not necessarily by the circle leader.*

11

Power-Building Exercises
for Sensitives

The healthiest bodies and the most balanced
minds and personalities among us already possess
a wealth of psychic and magnetic power. Generally
speaking, the fitter you are, the more vibrant is
your store of personal energy.

To keep your psychic energy-reserves in tip-top
condition: eat well; exercise regularly; sleep well;
try to remain as stress-free as possible; don't worry
unnecessarily, and take plenty of rest when you
need it. Balance your diet with the correct daily
intake of vitamins, proteins, minerals, and water,
and you will further increase your vitality.

Water and Personal Psychic Power

It's surprising how many millions of people don't
drink enough life-giving water.

A lack of water in the body can lead to all kinds of
complaints from constipation to general sluggish-
ness of the physical and mental make-up. Water is
an excellent conductor of electricity and of psychic
power. Psychically, if your body has its full quota of
water, your sensitivity to subtle energy-impulses
and spiritual forces will operate more efficiently.

The message is clear: drink more water.

Here's a general test to judge how much water your body needs each day: if your urine is a pale straw colour or is verging on the clear, your water intake is sufficient; but if your urine is dark green or deep yellow, your water intake is insufficient – so drink more water.

Here's a list of basic tips to help you to attain better health, and consequently to build up more personal psychic power:

Tips to Increase your Psychic Power

- Eat well, and follow a balanced diet.
- Drink clean spring-water, and not chemically-treated tapwater.
- Breathe pure, clean air.
- Don't allow yourself to become obese.
- Don't smoke or drink alcohol, or indulge in drug abuse: these activities dull the senses and damage the body's tissues.
- Take regular exercise, and don't be too inactive.
- Allow the sun's rays to invigorate your body.
- Rest whenever you need it, and obtain adequate sleep.
- Avoid stress; and don't rush around the world like a thing demented!
- Remain as calm and tranquil as possible within yourself.
- Prioritise your tasks, and don't worry about tomorrow.
- Spend a little time each day in meditation.
- Cultivate a loving and compassionate nature.
- Be tolerant, kind and thoughtful.
- Remove any bitterness and aggression from

your character.
- ♦ With a willing heart, offer service to all those who need it.
- ♦ Whenever possible, immerse yourself in the natural sounds of Nature.
- ♦ Bathe your spirit in the auric strength of trees, green fields, blue skies, and clear streams.
- ♦ Avoid harsh and discordant noises, and loud and aggressive people.
- ♦ Practice visualisation exercises to increase your personal psychic power.

Visualisation Exercises for Increasing your Psychic Power

Power-Building, Exercise One
Use this first visualisation if you need a general power-boost:
Sit quietly and calm your thoughts. Relax your body and close your eyes, then visualise yourself appearing in a familiar summer countryside scene, with a clear mountain river flowing by.

At the side of this beautiful river, remove your shoes and dangle your bare feet in the cool rushing water, and feel the pleasant sensation as it passes over your skin, cooling your feet.

Using the power of your imagination, draw up the water's invisible but powerful energy through the soles of your feet and then distribute it throughout your body.

Imagine that as the water-energy fills your body it cleanses you of all your impurities and tops-up your personal store of psychic power.

After a while, when you feel refreshed, return to

the Earthworld and ground yourself by opening your eyes and getting up and setting about your everyday chores again.

Power-Building, Exercise Two

If you feel lacking in strength or peace, you can do this exercise on a suitable piece of land, or from the comfort of your armchair simply by using the power of visualisation:

Find yourself a pleasant plot of land on which a tree is growing; you need to feel that this special tree is friendly towards you: it needs to be big and it should radiate power and peacefulness.

Sit comfortably and the foot of the tree, and feel the strength in its rough bark as you rest your back against its trunk. Close your eyes and listen to the sound of distant birdsong... then visualise the deep red energies of the earth, rising up into the tree and feeding it with red power.

Then draw up this power into your psychic self.

Breathe in the red energies of strength and power as if they were air, until they fill your auric energy-fields and you can sense them revitalising every fibre of your being.

Then open your eyes, and go back about your everyday business.

Power-Building, Exercise Three

Use this visualisation if you feel you have a mental or emotional imbalance:

Close your eyes and visit a field of green grass on a hot day by a shimmering crystal lake. Feel the heat of the sun beating down on your bare back, and listen to the sounds of the bees and birds as they wing their way around the wild flowers in the fields all around you.

Feel utterly at peace, in this, your own special place in the spirit countryside.

Remove the rest of your clothes and lie down on the soft, vibrant green grass and stare upwards at the clear electric-blue sky.

Feel the soft blades of grass as you intertwine them with your fingers.

Then relax...

Now close your spirit eyes and visualise the sun's rays as you draw them down into your psychic self. Breathe in the golden-white sunrays as if they were air, until they energise every fibre of your psychic being and you are glowing with psychic light.

Then relax again.

Take some deep and revitalising breaths, and feel at peace...

The colour green is right in the middle of the visible spectrum and it's linked with balance and harmony, so draw up into your spirit-body the green energy-light from within the grass, until you feel bathed and refreshed by its sense of harmony and balance.

Then, when you feel at peace, open your eyes and return to everyday life.

Power-Building, Exercise Four
Use this next exercise if you feel exhausted or nervously-depleted:
Within your special place in the spirit summer countryside, sit down on a large fallen log in the middle of a clearing surrounded by towering trees. Feel the rough bark of the log underneath the

palms of your hands, and listen to the gentle stirring of the breeze through the leaves all around you.

Gaze up at the vast green tree-canopy high above you, and watch the sun as it slowly enters the gap in the canopy overhead. Now you are lit by a column of brilliant sunlight.

Close your spirit eyes and draw down the golden-yellow, regenerating sunlight and direct it into your solar-plexus region, and then into the golden bowl of your mental aura.

Fill these auras with bright golden-yellow light, which is a quickening and enlivening energy.

Then, when you feel reinvigorated, open your eyes and return to the Earthworld and to everyday life.

12

Psychic Experimentation

Do you think psychic work, such as telepathic and psychometric experiments, should be practised in a development circle or an awareness class?

Yes, they're a good idea. Just like the body's muscles, a sensitive's dormant soul-powers need to be exercised in order to be strengthened.

However, experiments should be conducted toward the end of the class, after the silent time and the period when the sitters have shared the impressions they've received.

Here are some awareness exercises which may help you to increase your sensitivity:

Psychic Exercise One

Psychometry:

Select an object from a tray (a piece of jewellery, a bunch of keys, or any personal item), quieten your thoughts and then describe whatever psychic impressions you receive from it: speak about your feelings or the clairvoyant images you might see.

Don't get in the way of the thought-flow: with perfect trust, simply express whatever you perceive. Then, with your recipient's co-operation, test your degree of accuracy.

In time, you'll gain more experience and your accuracy rate will improve.

Variations on this Psychic Exercise

This same exercise can also be done by 'reading' a coloured ribbon or a flower that's been held by your recipient for a short while; or you could use a photograph concealed in an envelope. You could also select five playing-cards, place them face down and then try to psychically identify them before revealing their numbers and suits.

Or the leader could bring into the circle a mystery object belonging to someone outside the group, and you could try to read the impressions held within its energy-fields.

The leader could also bring in a stone from an ancient building or castle, and see if the sitters can glean from it any details of its past history.

Exercise your imagination and think up different ways to vary this basic format.

Psychic Exercise Two

Auric Reading:

Each member privately selects another person in the circle, and then tries to telepathically tune-in to the subject's auric energy-fields.

Try to be aware of the thoughts in the subject's mental bowl region, around the head.

See if you can do it.

You might receive significant impressions about your subject's thoughts or feelings, about his lifestyle, his hopes, desires, fears or aspirations. It's usually quite easy to register traumatic events in his past because powerful emotions impress themselves in the mind with greater intensity.

In all of these exercises, don't get in the way of the spontaneous thought-flow. Simply express whatever you perceive; and afterwards, with your recipient's co-operation, test your accuracy.

Eventually, you'll gain more fluency and your rate of accuracy will improve.

Psychic Exercise Three
'Blind' Auric Reading:

The circle leader selects a group member and blindfolds him, and then selects a sitter and places this person in front of the blindfolded psychic reader.

The reader then relays whatever impressions he receives from the sitter.

The sitter mustn't speak, for this would reveal his identity; only the leader is permitted to say 'Yes' or 'No', or 'We need more information'.

Afterwards, check your results meticulously.

Because this exercise removes all visual and aural contact between the psychic and his sitter, it helps to deepen the psychic's sensitivity.

Psychic Exercise Four
Telepathy:

Divide the circle into two groups.

The first group closes its eyes and the second group studies an object or photograph. The second group then tries to send images and thoughts about this object to the members of the first group.

This is a thought-transmission and -reception exercise; and if you think it sounds easy – try it!

Afterwards, the groups swap roles; and always

check the results thoroughly.

A Variation on this Exercise: The leader thinks of a sentence or an image and transmits it to the whole circle; after which the results are analysed. Or the leader places an object in a box and tries to transmit its shape and form to the group.

Psychic Exercise Five
Finding your Inner Voice:

While sitting in the silence, mentally recite a familiar piece of poetry or a prayer that you know by heart. The value of this exercise is that you become accustomed to hearing the sound of your own thought-voice.

It's surprising how many people never listen to themselves (let alone to anyone else).

If you don't know what your own thought-voice sounds like, how can you possibly distinguish it from the mind-voices of others?

Psychic Exercise Six
Scrying with a Crystal Ball, or with Water:

Using a clear glass or crystal sphere you can try to gaze into the future or peer into the past to seek answers to some of life's perplexing problems. If you don't have a sphere, take a small dark-coloured bowl, fill it with clear water, and you can gaze into the depths of that instead.

The ancient art of Crystal Gazing, or Scrying, can help to develop your natural soul-ability of clairvoyance. If you carefully follow the steps outlined beneath, with practice, patience and perseverance you might discover your power of second-sight:

♦ Scrying should be first attempted in a plain semi-darkened room. Sit with any subdued light behind you so that no light-shadows or furniture-shapes will fall upon the crystal ball or bowl of water. Don't attempt to scry after heavy work or after eating a meal, as these energy-burning activities might thwart your efforts.

♦ Make sure you won't be disturbed; and for ten minutes before you begin, sit comfortably and totally relax your mind and body. Breathe deeply several times, and try to feel at peace before scrying.

♦ Place a plain black cloth (preferably velvet) on your palm, and rest the crystal ball or bowl of water on it. To focus your attention, touch your forehead with the sphere or bowl – just above the bridge of your nose – then hold the object about nine to twelve inches from your eyes (or at a distance that feels comfortable to you).

♦ Look into the object...

♦ Don't stare hard or overstrain your eyes: try to become visually relaxed, so that you're gazing into the centre of the sphere (or into the depths of the water, beneath its surface) with slightly out-of-focus vision, as you look into what the ancients called the 'clear-deep'.

♦ Use the centre of the object as a focal point, but then try to look *through* the clear-deep, and to peer *beyond* it to reach a point in Infinity.

♦ Don't overstrain your sight – *relax your eyes*.

♦ Try this scrying exercise for about 15 minutes a

day, until you become accustomed to the psychic experience; and don't feel disappointed if at first you don't succeed – try again, because practice makes perfect.

♦ As your psychic sight gradually awakens and opens out, you might see a clouding within the ball or under the water (but, in fact, all visions occur only inside your mind; they just seem to be projected into the object). Some people see swirling colours; others see clouds and faces, or visions of people, or places or events.

Remember that any visions you might see will originate within your own mind; however, it's also possible that discarnate personalities might project their own telepathic pictures into your awareness.

Nevertheless, all clairvoyant visions should be analysed carefully.

If you ask a specific question and then scry and see an event, this doesn't mean you've seen the answer or witnessed the future or the past – it simply means you've observed a possible answer, or registered your own or someone else's thoughts about it.

Caution: Never, in any circumstances, cause anxiety or distress by revealing to clients unpleasant thoughts which can sometimes be seen. Read up on this subject and study as much material as you can, and always behave responsibly.

Always apply common sense and intelligence to any paranormal activity.

13

Working with the Public

Before we move on to examine in depth how to receive, place, and then deliver a successful spirit message, let's take a well-earned break from all our psychic activities and concentrate now on some essential guidelines about how to deal with the public in all kinds of situations.

Many tutors have misgivings about much of the work done by sensitives, particularly when these sensitives are psychic readers. A great deal of harm can be done when irresponsible or untrained psychics interact with the public, particularly when they fail to exercise due care and attention.

Counselling, and the Law of Personal Responsibility

There's a powerful spiritual law in the Universe. known as the Law of Personal Responsibility, which dictates that we are each responsible for whatever we think, say or do. *We* are responsible for making all the important decisions that chart our future courses, and no one else should attempt to make these decisions for us.

When I quote the following amusing, but very telling, story which appeared on a television comedy programme, I'm not being disrespectful to psychics – I'm making a serious point.

A mock news-announcer smiled and said, 'And now, for all our viewers who steadfastly refuse to take personal responsibility for their lives and for making their own decisions, we'll now pass you over to our resident psychic reader.'

Here are some important questions which all sensitives should try to answer to their own satisfaction:

♦ Why do people want psychic readings?
♦ Why do psychics serve the public?
♦ Why do people want private appointments for mediumship or healing treatments?
♦ Why do mediums and spiritual healers offer their services to the public?
♦ What is the purpose of offering mediumship, psychic readings, or healing to the public?

The Purpose of Psychic Readings

Responsible psychics claim that their work can:

♦ Make their clients aware of the Law of Personal Responsibility.
♦ Help their clients to recognise the potential for greater happiness and fulfilment.
♦ Demonstrate to their clients that ESP (Extra-Sensory Perception) can operate, and that their thoughts can be seen and 'read'.
♦ Help their clients to make choices about taking right-action in their lives.
♦ Offer their clients a set of future possibilities and pathways to think about.
♦ Give their clients reassurance about their lines of

thought (which is a form of counselling).
+ Encourage their clients to examine and reassess their personal conditions and their lives.
+ Offer their clients a sensible referral service (e.g. encourage them to see a family doctor, surgeon, psychiatrist, or to seek other professional help).

Some of the Dangers Involved in Giving Private Consultations and Treatments

In support of all sensitives, their work can help the public to focus their minds on a range of possible directions or solutions to their problems, and psychic messages might help clients to chose new lifestyles.

A mediumistic contact can remove the fear of death, and can offer evidence of an Afterlife.

Spiritual Healing can bring relief from pain and suffering and can awaken in patients' souls an awareness of the Divine Spark of God that lies within them.

All kinds of psychic consultations offer evidence that the brain is not the seat of consciousness, and that we are more than just flesh and blood.

All of these aims are admirable and positive, but the reality can be quite different, for untrained and irresponsible sensitives are in constant danger of falling into the following hazardous traps:

+ They frequently offer life-counselling, without having any qualifications or training in these skills.
+ They often contravene the Law of Personal Responsibility by telling their clients which

pathways they should take, and what decisions they should make.

+ They sometimes glean their clients' futures, but offer these impressions as definite pathways rather than as sets of possibilities.

+ They sometimes diagnose emotional, mental, and physical health conditions without the slightest medical training or professional qualifications. (In Britain, at present, it is illegal to diagnose illnesses unless you're a qualified doctor or veterinary surgeon.)

+ They often promise that some of the client's crippling personal circumstances will soon be cured, released, or resolved.

+ And some sensitives charge exorbitant fees for their services. (I'll discuss the contentious issue of payment later on.)

All of these dangers apply to every sensitive, but it's the psychic readers who commit the greatest number of transgressions on a private, one-to-one basis; particularly when giving telephone psychic readings, or Internet consultations by e-mail, or by videophone etc.

In their private readings many psychics often concentrate on a few key areas of their client's lives, and these are:

+ **Relationships**: lovers; romantic attachments; friends, family, spouses; quarrels and divorces etc.

+ **Money**: financial security, or insecurity.

+ **Career**: work, and significant changes ahead.

+ **Desires**: wishes, dreams and hopes; luck and good fortune.

- **Fears**: anxious situations; 'magical' charms and spells to ward off misfortune, etc.
- **Health**: physical, emotional and mental conditions.

It's easy to see why some people seek the services of psychic readers; generally, they want these two questions answered: *'What will my future be? And can you tell me what I should do?'*

And the psychic's answer to both these questions should be: *'I can't be sure of your future; and if I told you what to do I'd be breaking the Law of Personal Responsibility.'*

Sadly, many psychics do break these guidelines; and a number of mediums and healers are also guilty of this charge.

Even when working at their best levels, psychics usually relay back to their sitters what's already in their minds; and sometimes they touch upon a misty set of future possibilities.

Ideally, no sensitives should break the Law of Personal Responsibility by attempting to answer questions such as:

- *When will my divorced husband come back to me?*
- *Will I win the Lottery draw this year? Can you give me the correct numbers?*
- *When will I sell my house, and will I get the asking-price?*
- *Do you think I should leave my children and make a new life of my own?*
- *Can you give me a lucky charm to keep evil influences away from me?*
- *Can you cure my health condition?*

And so on, *ad infinitum*.

Forecasting the Future

All sensitives, but particularly psychic readers, should be wary of forecasting the future.

How do you know that what you clairsentiently sense or clairvoyantly see will actually occur?

Only time will tell, and you should acknowledge this. Exceptionally few psychics are certain of the accuracy of their predictions because forecasting the future with any degree of accuracy is an extremely rare ability.

The only way you can perfect this skill is to rigorously work at it and test it privately:

- *Try to forecast the exact wording of tomorrow's newspaper headlines.*
- *Walk down an unfamiliar road and, before you actually see it, describe the last house in the row.*
- *Try to foresee what will happen to a family member in the next forty-eight hours (but only with his permission, of course).*
- *Select a house near yours, and try to forecast what changes there might be in its appearance in the next three days (different curtains, a bike left outside the door, new plantpots, etc).*
- *Try to pick the winner in horse race.*
- *Try to forecast the results of a competition.*
- *Try to foresee what photographs might be taken at a forthcoming family event (at a party or a wedding, or on a daytrip, etc).*
- *Test your psychic perception by trying to read face-down playing-cards.*

- *Forecast how many flowerheads will appear on your favourite plant.*
- *Try to describe the contents of tomorrow's mail. How many letters will you receive? What's in them?*

If you think any of the above psychic skills is easy, you're very much mistaken. And if you can't do these tests and achieve a high degree of accuracy of at least 70-80%, what makes you think you can foresee someone else's future?

This is a thought-provoking question to which all psychics should give their serious consideration.

'Beware the Ides of March!'
Don't be a prophet of doom and gloom, irresponsibly foretelling deaths and other tragedies with positivity. This is dangerous ground, indeed.

Guard Your Tongue Well
Whatever kind of spiritual work you do, you should always avoid giving irresponsible advice, and you should never counsel a member of the public unless you're professionally qualified to do so. To highlight this point, here's a true story.

One night in a busy hospital, a nurse tucked into bed an elderly woman, who happened to remark, 'My index finger feels a bit sore today, nurse'; to which the nurse casually, and unthinkingly, replied, 'Oh, I expect that's a bit of arthritis setting in.'

The patient immediately became anxious, then fearful, and then began screaming uncontrollably. She couldn't be calmed and had to be sedated. The nurse was severely reprimanded for making what the patient believed was a diagnosis.

The patient had become hysterical because her deceased mother had been wheelchair-bound through acute rheumatoid arthritis, which had started in one of her fingers and had progressed from there to paralyse her body for several years before her death.

When the elderly patient was told that her own finger-pain was 'probably a bit of arthritis setting in', she immediately feared the same fate as her mother.

There are two important teaching-points in this true story.

First: the nurse should have remained silent and kept her opinions to herself; or perhaps she might have offered some sensible and comforting advice such as, 'Why not have a word with the doctor about it tomorrow?'

And second: distress can often be caused not by the ordinary words that you speak, but by the mind into which they enter.

Guard your tongue well.

How many sensitives intimately know the clients to whom they deliver messages?

How many sensitives can predict what kind of reaction their words might cause in a vulnerable or anxious mind?

The answer is clear: no sensitive can be certain of the contents of another person's mind; therefore, tread carefully and speak wisely. Listen graciously and offer your sympathy and empathy, but keep your opinions to yourself.

The Vulnerability of Sitters

Critics of sensitives are quite right to consistently point out the vulnerability of sitters.

The kinds of people who might seek out your help will vary tremendously. Among them will be the grieving, the curious, the cynical, the unbelieving, the mildly interested, the mentally unstable, the emotionally vulnerable, the irrepressible fanatics, the physically ill – and many others.

Every sitter should be treated with respect.

Try to imagine how you'd feel if a sensitive spoke to you in public about your deeply personal life. Put yourself in the other man's shoes, and you will see why it's so important to respect his dignity.

An arrogant medium was once reprimanded when she was rather crudely accused of 'ramming her message down a recipient's throat'. When it was explained that she was probably dealing with a grieving, vulnerable woman, and that she should therefore be more sympathetic, her reply was, 'But she wasn't accepting my message.'

In no circumstances should any sensitive follow this woman's appalling example of how to treat a member of the public.

Be compassionate and tolerant, and exercise understanding and restraint at all times.

Frequency of Consultations or Treatments

Some vulnerable sitters who find it difficult to come to terms with the circumstances in their lives regularly resort to mediums, psychics, and healers to help them through these crises; but sensitives shouldn't allow themselves to become 'emotional crutches'. What these kinds of distressed sitters might need is professional life-counselling, or Cognitive Behavioural Therapy.

Sensitives shouldn't give consultations to the same sitters too frequently; however, in the case of spiritual healers and other kinds of complementary therapists, patients may need to be seen on a weekly basis until improvement is noted.

Success Rates and Promises

No genuine medium or psychic can guarantee that a consultation will be successful. The success rates will vary according many conditions which govern the work: your health, the client's health, the psychic and spiritual conditions in and around the séance-room, all of these factors, and more, can affect the results, and sometimes dramatically.

Any medium who claims he can contact specific entities whenever he chooses is either deluded or he's a charlatan. You can send out mental requests to communicators to attend a consultation, but you can't guarantee success.

A mediumistic sitting could surprise you and be dominated by a drop-in communicator; that is, a communicator who may not even belong to the sitter's family, but who might be known to his relatives, neighbours or friends.

Drop-in communicators can often provide some startling evidence of survival once their statements have been placed and carefully checked.

The Right to Privacy and Confidentiality

You clients have a right to expect privacy and confidentiality, and you should never discuss their business with anyone else; except, of course, with another sensitive whose advice you may require if your client has problems you're unqualified to deal with – and even then you shouldn't name your client: you should discuss only the problem.

Subjects to Avoid when
Giving Messages in Public

There are some obvious subjects you should avoid mentioning when working in public, because a crowd of witnesses is avidly listening to your client's business. How would you feel if a sensitive began delving into your own personal life in front of a crowd of people, and then ventured into some of the following areas?

- **Sex**: your sexual preferences and activities, and your personal relationships.
- **Finances**: how much money you may, or may not, have.
- **Politics**: a divisive subject at the best of times.
- **Religion**: another topic which makes people very hot under the collar.
- **All Kinds of Bad News**: tragedies, accidents, impending divorces, health difficulties, deaths approaching, etc.
- **The Future**: no one can be certain that what is 'seen' will subsequently occur.

If you're a medium, you should be particularly careful not to allow communicators to lead you into the deep and often muddy waters of your recipients' personal lives.

Let's take a look now at some other problems that might affect you and your work.

Uncontrolled Sensitivity

You should be the master of your abilities. You alone decide when you'll work and when you'll stop. Don't be an uncontrolled sensitive, or as a friend of mind rather amusingly says, 'Don't be a leaky psychic!'

Be strong-minded and exercise discipline. 'Open up' your awareness, work with it, and then 'close it down' by getting on with everyday life and not giving psychic matters a second thought.

The Need for Spiritual Strength

There's a power about which many sensitives often remain unaware, and this is the need to generate within themselves a battery of soul-strength. No sensitive person could possibly survive the stresses and trials of modern life without a well-disciplined mind.

Without doubt, mental strength is an essential part of any soul's spiritual armour, so you should acquire it.

Unchecked, a man's thoughts tend to gallop out of control like wild unbroken stallions; but to achieve and maintain inner harmony and peace – and therefore establish a state of contentment – he must learn to rein in the wild horses of Thought, or nothing but chaos will rule his life.

Sensitive people should become the masters of their minds if they wish to progress spiritually.

The mind should be man's servant, and not his tyrant.

But there is no instant soul evolution: by its very nature spiritual progression is a gradual advance from the lower state towards the higher, from the less aware towards the more sensitive.

You alone are responsible for changing your attitudes; you alone must resolve to be a happier and more balanced soul.

You can be advised, helped and counselled by others, certainly, and this guidance and inspiration is always available from people in both worlds, but the task of changing your outlook is yours.

Earth is a temporary training-ground into in which souls are born in order to evolve their spiritual natures: it's a grounding-place meant for learning and growing. Earth is a plane of existence where you'll be presented with opportunities to expand your awareness and develop your character through the expression of your personality.

A well developed, balanced spiritual personality resembles a fine silk thread: it should possess a sensitivity and responsiveness to the multifarious vibrations of life around it, and yet this seemingly delicate thread should also be as strong as flexible steel wire.

Fees, Fame, and Fortune

If you intend to use your skills to become famous or wealthy, re-examine your motivation.

I can't advise sensitives whether or not to charge for their services: that's a matter for each person's conscience. It's your decision.

But there's nothing wrong with receiving a fair day's pay for a fair day's work.

However, here are a few thoughts to consider: if you walk into a baker's shop, ask for a loaf of bread and then pay for it, you'll receive a loaf of bread. If it's fit for human consumption, all is well; but if it isn't, you can ask for your money back, and you should receive it in full.

Bear this principle in mind.

If a person comes to you for a consultation, what exactly can you offer them?

You can give them your time and also the benefit of your professional skills, along with your loving concern, but you cannot ever guarantee successful results. Any sensitive who guarantees success, particularly when money is involved, is a deluded person or, worse still, a charlatan or confidence trickster.

I sincerely hope you're not one of these.

*

In the following chapters, we'll now continue our studies together by examining more closely, and in greater depth, the subject of mediumship, concentrating mainly on its quality and on the construction and content of spirit messages that are given to the public.

14

How to Achieve
Mediumistic Attunement

Let's look more closely at what mediums are supposed to do when they've entered the silence in a circle. If you're a medium or a spiritual healer, how can you establish contact with people living in the Beyond? The process can be summed up in one word: 'attunement', in all its aspects.

Mediumistic attunement is closely linked with psychic sensitivity. Mediumship occurs when a medium's mind-frequencies approximate the thought-wavelengths of his communicators in the spirit world. In your development circle you should learn how to focus, sharpen, and heighten your mental awareness. Your thought-processes should be formed into what ancient mystics termed 'the single-pointed mind'.

At the point of contact, mediums must learn to forget about the Earthworld and their earthly cares and then 'open up' their awareness to the people in the world of spirit, and then concentrate on working with them until the job is done.

The art of becoming attuned to the vibrations of the next world is learned through private communication taking place in the silence, and through practising your skills and gaining experience.

Your mind can be divided into three levels: the conscious, subconscious, and superconscious. It's in the superconscious mind that your contact with the world of spirit is registered, but it reaches you through your subconscious mind, after which it then dawns in your consciousness.

The superconscious mind is always in touch with eternity, and you must learn to become more aware of this vibrant yet subtle level of thought.

Having entered into the silence, remain mentally wide awake and aware (don't fall asleep!); you should be in full control of your faculties, while at the same time trying to heighten your perceptions.

Try listening, or registering, the sensations of any discarnate presences nearby. Listen carefully for the 'still, small thought-voice', which is frequently the flickering beginning of subjective (or intuitive) clairaudience (clear-hearing): the more objective (almost physical-sounding) spirit tones usually manifest later when your inner senses have deepened and heightened more expansively.

With your eyes closed (which removes visual impressions of the Earthworld), drift into a pleasant feeling of daydreaming or of 'building castles in the air'.

Relax, and enjoy the peace...

Remove all tension from your eyes, throat and solar-plexus regions – too much tension in these three chakra-points can often 'block out' your awareness of the spirit world's subtle vibrations.

If you wish, you can briefly focus your attention on your chakras and auras and try to expand their energy-fields. You could visualise yourself filled with psychic light, and then instruct yourself to be ready to receive communication through the extended photosphere of sensitivity all around you.

Then, notice and enjoy viewing any pictures or scenes that float through your awareness.

If you see, sense, or hear any spirit visitors, ask them to remain close and then enter into mental communication with them.

Invite them to speak to you. And then *listen*.

I cannot say this too often: *mediums must learn to listen the spirit world*.

Try to register the thoughts and feelings that the spirit people bring with them into the séance-room. Pay attention to any pictures, feelings, ideas, or streams of thought that begin to flow into your awareness, or are reflected upon the mirror of your mind.

Remain passive and be open to contact; wait patiently, and positively expect success.

If the seeds of mediumship are ready to flower within you, you will experience results.

Patience is a virtue.

Practice makes perfect.

No one can develop these subtle skills for you.

Later, at the end of the silence, you can relay to the group any philosophical thoughts, messages, or guidance that your inspirers communicated to you.

Does anything else happen in the circle's quiet time?

Within the mighty power of the silence, healing powers might develop within you. Spirit healing guides often take this golden opportunity to tune-in to your auric fields and mind, and they might project specialised healing-rays through your energy-fields to others in the circle, or to others outside in the world.

It is we who limit the power of the spirit: our slow and often ponderous physical consciousness frequently prevents, blocks, incorrectly interprets, or colours much of what our spirit friends transmit to us.

Nevertheless, you will be guided and inspired (often imperceptibly) along your path of psychic and spiritual unfoldment.

The spirit people do a great deal of unseen work in order to reach us so that they can deliver their communications and their philosophy. We remain largely passive until we receive their links, and then we become more active when we try to deliver them proficiently.

*

When I was a younger medium, I asked my spirit guides for more clarity of attunement, pinpoint accuracy and unquestionable evidence of survival to be given in our work.

As there so often is when listening-in to the spirit world, there was a long silence; but eventually an answer came.

A spirit voice replied, 'We're already transmitting precise facts to you, young man, but you're not yet sensitive enough to perceive them.

'*You* must develop your sensitivity: it's your ability, and it's your responsibility. We can quicken it, advise and guide you in your development, but only you can sharpen your mental faculties.

'If you wish to register us with greater clarity, remember that the gifts of the Spirit are not given or easily won: they must be earned, treasured, nurtured, and then carefully polished and maintained in perfect working order by their possessor, and not by us.'

I was startled.

In the long struggle to attain perfect attunement with the spirit people, not one of us can ever claim to be fully developed. As each new hard-earned feather adorns our mediumistic caps, several other unexpected challenges rise before us, waiting to be met.

Such is the pattern of life; and such is the pattern of the development of mediumship.

We hear a great deal about the poor standards of mediumship these days, but if the standards are low then the fault lies squarely with us, and not with our inspirers.

As far as your psychic and spiritual development are concerned: the buck stops with you. And here's another truism for your consideration:

You cannot buy experience.

As a medium, whether you stand before twenty people or two thousand and twenty and claim a link with another world, if your link falters or becomes unclear, no one on Earth will help you to put it right.

Although the spirit people do a great deal more of the hard work than we do, we must accept the responsibility for heightening our perceptions.

15

Developing Mental Mediumship Skills
Getting the Message Across with
The CERT Formula

How can I tell the difference between the thoughts or images that are reaching me from the spirit world, and my own thoughts?
Experience is your teacher here, but remember that if the spirit world projects into your mind, let us say, an image of a house, it's usually a sharp and clear-cut picture. The image is usually quite bright, the colours are vibrant, and its details are clearly perceived.

However, if you create your own mental image of a house, you must take time to construct it (it doesn't appear instantaneously as spirit images do), and your picture won't not be as clearly defined as a spirit vision is.

How can I discover if the paranormal facts I'm receiving are coming from a discarnate source or purely from a psychic one? Can you offer me any guidance?
Yes, I can. For the last three decades I've taught the following formula to innumerable mediums and, even though I've now witnessed other tutors

147

using it to train their own development classes, I claim the copyright here!

In all mediumistic messages, a communicator must be present; and all genuine mediumistic messages usually conform to a pattern that I've called the CERT formula, which stands for:

C = Communicator.
E = Evidence of identity.
R = Reason for the spirit-return.
T = Tie up all the loose ends.

Every spirit message of survival evidence should contain these four elements.

Please explain more fully each part of your CERT formula.
Let's start from the top:

Communicator:

A communicator must be present: this will be a man, a woman, a child, or an animal. Mediums must be certain that an invisible entity is trying to communicate with them: they might hear his voice clairaudiently, see his spirit form clairvoyantly, sense his presence clairsentiently, or simply receive a stream of thought from him.

Sometimes these four skills work simultaneously, but at other times (because sensitivity fluctuates) perhaps only one, or two, of these abilities may operate; but, ideally, mediums shouldn't start relaying a spirit message unless they're certain they're in touch with a spirit communicator.

If you don't know whether or not you're linking

with a living spirit entity who radiates a vibrant, separate personality, then you're not a medium – and it's back into the development class for you.

Evidence:
The discarnate person must give you some positive information that will identify him or her.

I mean accurate statements that spring from the communicator's mind: spirit people are warm and emotional beings and their messages are full of individual character and feeling.

Some of the details they often transmit are: their passing; their names; their relationship to the recipient; their family details; quaint phrases they used when on Earth; and significant memories that unquestionably link them with their loved ones.

Reason for Return:
The reason for the spirit-return should always be stated. Every communicator has something to say to those he loves on Earth.

If a medium is truly in contact with a personality on the Other Side of Life, he will receive the *reason* why that communicator is present. The reason for the spirit-return is probably the most important part of a spirit message.

Tie-up the Loose Ends:
Don't be the kind of medium who delivers a mishmash of confusing information that is often accompanied by the tiresome advice to, 'Take it home and think about it!'

From today onwards, accept that it is part of your responsibility to relay intelligent and acceptable messages, and to make sense of as many of their details as you can, there and then, at the time of their transmission.

Spirit messages shouldn't confuse people: they should clarify their thoughts.

If your communicator suddenly mentions a pushbike and this reference isn't understood by your recipient, don't let the subject drop: ask your guide for more information. Then continue with the link, but return to that errant bike at the end of the message and clarify its significance.

Tie-up all the loose ends.

(Don't leave that poor bike outside in the rain: it'll get rusty! And it needs to be in good working order because we'll need it later, as you'll see.)

'Please', 'Thank you', and 'I Don't Know':
These are six little words that all sensitives should use quite frequently.

*

Could you provide an example of a mediumistic message in which all the elements of the CERT formula are clearly in evidence?
The following spirit message which I delivered on tour, and which was reported in *Psychic News*, conforms to the CERT formula:

Stephen began by asking to speak to 'a young lady with the surname of Edwards. I have here a young man who recently passed into the spirit world.'

The woman was quickly located and the medium informed her, 'Your fiancé is with me. His name is

David.'

She was clearly taken aback. 'Yes.'

'It was a tragic passing, and a sudden transition.'

'Yes it was.'

When Stephen heard the boy saying 'Alison', the recipient confirmed that this was her name; and when he sent his love to Carl and Wayne, she said that these were his two younger brothers who could not attend the meeting on that night.

The medium then relayed the cause of the communicator's death.

'He says he was driving a high-powered Honda motorbike – it was a new machine that he'd only just bought – but it crashed into the back of a lorry.'

The young woman was so moved by the message that she only managed to whisper 'Yes' through the microphone.

Recognising his recipient's grief, Stephen took great care to proceed gently as he described further aspects of David's life and personality.

'Despite the fact that he was a Hell's Angel, he says he was quite a sensitive chap. He used to play the piano, and he liked to listen to opera – especially to Maria Callas.'

This, too, was accepted.

Unknown to the medium, the communicator then drew the rest of his family into the message.

Stephen reported: 'David tells me that the last thing he said to his mother on the day of the crash was, "Don't wait up for me tonight, mum, I'm going to be very late indeed."'

The lad's mother, who was sitting next to his father and his fiancée, tearfully verified this statement, and further accepted her son's

STEPHEN O'BRIEN

assurance that he 'very much liked the new black-and-white picture' of him, 'which is hanging over the fireplace.'

The medium then relayed a wealth of love to David's family, correctly giving the lad's age of death as 19, and the fact that 'the accident took place just before a crossroads on a narrow country road. It was a rainy day, and visibility was poor.'

Then came an unusual piece of survival evidence.

Stephen said, 'Your son is aware that there was some disagreement in the family about the floral tribute for his funeral.'

Pointing to the lad's fiancée, the medium said, 'you wanted his name made up of flowers,' and then to the father he said, 'but your idea won the day, Dad!'

The boy's father called out, 'It did.'

The young communicator then used Stephen's clairaudience to deliver a startling piece of evidence.

'David wants me to tell you that he loved the floral tribute, which was shaped into the form of a three-dimensional crash-helmet.'

The boy's family were clearly astonished and his emotional mother replied, 'That's quite correct. We thank you. Thank you so much.'

How can mediums obtain detailed information from their communicators?

Mediums should always strive to receive more and more precise facts: don't be lazy and just 'give what you get and be satisfied'. Progress comes when mediums realise that they must expand the boundaries of their abilities.

Ask your communicators for more information:

communicate with them!

If you're truly in touch with discarnate entities they will respond. And *listen* to your spirit friends; people seem to have lost the art of how to listen attentively. You must develop, sharpen, unfold and refine your psychic faculties; the spirit people will help you, of course, but your talents strengthen only through use and intelligent application and analysis.

If you look for accurate details, you're more likely to receive them.

Wishy-washy descriptions and vague feelings and sensations are the hallmarks of an undeveloped sensitive.

If precise details are absent from a medium's demonstration, then the medium shouldn't be on the public platform: he should return to the development class.

How can I train myself to improve my ability to receive thoughts from the next world, rather than to receive impressions from people living in this one?

There are several exercises to help you learn the difference between receiving mediumistic and psychic impressions. Here are some, which should be done only in a private class: an unsuspecting public shouldn't be practised upon!

Mediumistic Exercises

Exercise for Improving Your Clairvoyance, Clairaudience, and Clairsentience Skills

You can do this exercise when you're sitting in the

quietness of your circle.

Spend a little time to test these three senses in turn. To improve your clairaudience, invite your guides to come within your auric sphere of sensation and ask them to speak to you – and then you must *listen*.

Do the same test with your clairvoyance: ask your guides to show you pictures or symbols, and mentally describe to them exactly what you see, so that they can ascertain if their transmissions are getting through clearly.

Then test your clairsentience by sensing the different presences near to you: your guides might bring a dog or cat, or a child, close to your auric fields. See if you can 'sense' the personalities of these beings. And while you're in communication, why not strike up a conversation with your spirit visitors and try to develop all of your abilities simultaneously?

Exercise One; Blindfold Mediumship

Select a medium in your group, blindfold him, and then face him away from the rest of the class.

Next, get him to establish a mental link with a spirit communicator and ask him to deliver a message, remembering that it should conform to the CERT formula.

The medium isn't allowed to select his recipient from the group, which helps to rule out a telepathic link being made; instead, he listens only to his spirit inspirer.

Once the link has begun, the only two people allowed to speak are the medium and the class tutor: the tutor takes complete control of the acceptance or refusal of any information given.

Recipients mustn't respond vocally, they should simply nod to the leader, who says only 'Yes,' 'No,' 'Maybe,' or 'We need more information on that,' until the link is completed, and the CERT formula had been fulfilled.

Another class member should write down all the information supplied, and afterwards each detail should be checked or researched.

Each medium should be put through his paces like this.

Exercise Two; Homework Mediumship
Each circle member secretly writes down his name plus a selection of random numbers on a piece of paper, which he hands to the leader.

The leader then asks each member to do a private mediumistic reading for the set of numbers that he allocates to him. (The mediums mustn't know who their recipients are.)

Only when physically alone, in the silence of his own home, does each medium tune in to the spirit world, then he writes down a few pages of spirit-supplied evidence intended for the recipient.

At the next gathering, the leader matches up each medium with his recipient, and every piece of information is thoroughly checked and verified.

In this way, the mediums are taught to recognise, and then to rely solely upon, the voice of the spirit world.

Exercise Three; Mystery Guest Mediumship
On a special evening, halfway through the circle a mystery guest is admitted. No introductions are

made, and the guest must remain silent.

Each member of the group then tunes-in to the spirit world to receive a mediumistic message for the visitor, ensuring that it contains the elements of the CERT formula.

The information is written down in silence, and afterwards it is accepted or rejected by the guest.

Caution: Don't choose a guest who is vulnerable to suggestion, for your students will make mistakes.

To test the circle to its limits, why not invite a Polish or German visitor? This could be a good way of encouraging the development of clairaudience!

Exercise Four; Proxy Sittings

The leader compiles a list of knowledgeable sitters (from outside the circle) who are willing to receive survival messages, but none of these is allowed to attend the group.

On circle night, the leader asks each member to write down a mediumistic message for a specific sitter, which should contain ten factual statements conforming to the CERT formula. But a *nom-de-plume* is given to each sitter. For example, Dorothy Prince becomes Mr Poole; Mrs Hamish is called Professor Yale; and Miss Taylor becomes Mr Jenkins, etc.

After the circle, the leader collects the sheets of written evidence, and the following week they are returned to the mediums, each fact having been ticked or marked as correct or incorrect.

(Note: the leader should meet the sitters and verbally check each statement himself, which affords him the opportunity to eliminate any statement that

might cause upset.)

Caution: *The mediums must write only statements of fact: no questions are allowed. One mark should be given for each correct statement, to obtain a total out of ten. To obtain the medium's percentage of accuracy, simply add a nought to this figure. For example: six correct statements out of ten means the medium has achieved 60% accuracy.*

An acceptable degree of accuracy for a reliable medium would be in the region of 70-80%, or higher.

These are quite tough but excellent awareness exercises, and if only more circles would adopt these kinds of strict training methods, the standard of mediumship would rise dramatically overnight.

16

Getting and Delivering a Spirit Contact in Public

Whenever you work in public as a medium, your first responsibility is to obtain a spirit contact.

Once you've quietened your thoughts, you should then invite your spirit helpers to link with you – and then SENSE, LOOK and LISTEN.

Symbols and Sensations

In the early stages of your work you might see only symbols or be aware only of vague sensations or presences around you. You might be fortunate enough to hear a communicator's thought-voice in your mind, or even a spirit voice that sounds quite objective, as if the person were standing in the room next to you.

If you do receive symbols, try to understand what they might mean.

For example: the spirit people might project onto the mirror of your mind a picture of a King, and give you the sensation of a woman's presence nearby. Perhaps the woman's name is Miss King, but you couldn't hear her when she spoke to you.

The spirit people will try any avenue to reach you successfully.

Persevere.

I remember in my early days seeing a spirit woman so clearly that I can still describe the homely old dear today; however, she obviously couldn't make herself heard because she stood in front of me holding up a piece of paper, on which she'd written: *I'm Gladys!*

The more you use your abilities, the more they will strengthen and improve.

But it's important when you're working to remain *aware*. You must try to be aware of what is passing through your mind. You should pay attention to whatever pictures or images you see; you should remember the written words that appear on the mirror of your mind, listen to any thoughts or spirit voices that speak to you, and acknowledge any spirit presences nearby.

Then describe what you can see, sense or hear.

As a medium you must be a faithful reporter.

'Colouring' the Communications

When delivering a link, you shouldn't try to interpret it too precisely, or to weave an interesting story around the spirit-supplied facts, or to make the message sound 'impressive': you should give exactly what you receive, nothing more and nothing less.

And you shouldn't make assumptions about your communicators or state facts that you haven't been given. For example, if you see an elderly lady, say so; don't say, 'I can see an elderly lady who looks about sixty-eight.' If she doesn't tell you her age – don't guess it.

Always avoid the desire to 'colour' your spirit-information. Don't change the message or alter it in any way. And don't allow your recipients to change the details of your message, either.

With the greatest of respect, most recipients wouldn't be able to tell you what they'd had for breakfast on that morning, never mind what they'd done fifty years ago! If you allow them to, your recipients will lead you up the garden path. Don't allow them to do it.

And don't 'make the details fit', either. Always follow your inspirers' lines of thought, and trust them; and stick to the facts you're given unless the spirit people themselves decide to change them.

Imagine if you were a spirit communicator: how would you feel if a medium changed the message you were trying to give? Or if a medium guessed your age incorrectly by ten years?

Your loved one might be sitting in the crowd and thinking, 'That sounds exactly like my friend in the spirit world, but it can't be because the age is wrong' – and your message might never be delivered or accepted.

Placing your Link
The art of speaking to the public, while at the same time tuning-in and listening to the people in the spirit world, isn't an easy skill: but with practice you'll master it.

If your information is vague – and it *shouldn't* be if you're appearing in public – you'll have great difficulty in placing your message with the correct recipient.

For example: if you simply state: *'I have an elderly lady with me; she had white hair, and she*

died of a heart-attack. Does anyone know her?' –
you don't have enough detailed information to
locate the correct recipient.

Even if your communicator actually points to
where her relative is sitting in the crowd and
you're able to address that recipient, as it stands
your message doesn't contain sufficient evidential
information. If this is the kind of spirit message
you're used to delivering, then you should return
to the development class.

Now let us follow this simple message as it builds
up from its unacceptable state until it reaches a
state of excellence, and we'll clearly see the high
standard to which all mediums should aspire.

Incidentally, if you're already a medium you can
compare the quality of your own work against that
in the following example:

Unacceptable
*'I have an elderly lady with me; she had white
hair and she died of a heart-attack. Does anyone
know her?'*

Poor
*'I have an elderly lady with me; she had white
hair and she died of a heart-attack. She wants to
contact a relative, a woman in here tonight. Does
anyone know her?'*

Fair
*'I have an elderly lady with me; she had white
hair and she died of a heart-attack in her
seventies. She wants to contact a woman in here
tonight, a daughter of hers. Does anyone know*

the name of Gladys?'

Good/Acceptable

'I have an elderly lady with me called Gladys; she had white hair, and she died of a heart-attack in her seventies. She wants to contact her daughter, and I get the name of Simpson connected with this woman. Does anyone with the surname of Simpson recognise this elderly lady?'

Very Good

'I have an elderly lady with me, called Gladys Phillips. She had snow-white hair and was in her seventies when she died of a heart-attack, at home. She gives me a strong impression of the stairs in her house. And she says she wants to contact her daughter, whose name is Janet Simpson. Is there a lady called Janet Simpson here tonight, please?'

Excellent

'I have an elderly white-haired lady here with me: her name is Gladys Phillips and she was 78 years old when she died at home of a massive heart-attack. She tells me that her daughter found her body at the foot of the stairs, next to the kitchen door.

'She says her daughter's here tonight, and that her name is Janet Simpson. I'm told you're sitting in the front row of the gallery.' (Then point to the correct person and say:) *'Please speak up Mrs Simpson: I have a message from your mother tonight.'*

(Note: *no questions were asked of the recipient.)*

This excellent start of a mediumistic message identifies the **Communicator** and the recipient by their full names, and it also contains other pieces of evidence (the manner of passing; the location of the body and who found it, etc).

But now we must complete the link by delivering the rest of the elements of the **CERT** formula; that is, we should try to obtain more **Evidence** of the person who is communicating, and then supply the **Reason** for their spirit-return. Finally, we should complete the message by **Tying-up all the loose ends**.

Delivering the Rest of the Message

As we did in the previous example, we'll follow the progression of the message from its unacceptable state to its state of excellence:

Unacceptable
'I feel that your daughter is concerned about something. Have you been feeling ill?'

Poor
'I feel that your daughter is concerned about you and her family. I think she has some children. And have you been feeling ill?'

Fair
'Your daughter's concerned about you, and about her family: I think she has three boys. She says you've been feeling ill recently, and that you've visited the doctor.

Good/Acceptable

'Your daughter's concerned about you, and about her family. She says she has three boys and that they miss her terribly. She still cares for them, and visits them each day. Please tell them this.

'She also knows that you've been to the doctor's recently. She says she went with you, and he prescribed some blood-pressure tablets for you.

'Keep taking them.

'And your daughter's also giving me a strong impression about someone "wanting a pushbike".'

Very Good

'Your daughter's concerned about you, and about her family. She says she has three sons, all young boys, and that they're missing her terribly. She wants you to tell them she's still alive, and that she cares for them deeply. She visits them each day, and their father, too. Please tell the whole family this.

'She also knows you've been to the doctor's recently and that he prescribed a course of blood-pressure tablets for you. "Keep taking the tablets, Mum!" she says. And she's also remembering something about wanting to buy a new bicycle for her youngest son, whose name is Joseph.'

Excellent

'Your daughter's concerned about you, and about her family. She says she has three young sons, all boys, and they're missing her terribly. She wants you to tell them she's still alive, and that she cares for them deeply. She sends her love to them: their names are Michael, John and Joseph. The youngest one, Joseph, is particularly grieving for *her. Tell him that she's fine in the Other World.*

'She visits them all each day, including their father, whose name is Albert. Please send her love to the whole family.

'She also knows that you went to the doctor's last Tuesday (because she went with you) and he prescribed a course of blood-pressure tablets for you. She says, "You've been skipping two of them each day, and you're not following your doctor's orders to rest in the afternoon. Keep taking the tablets, Mum!"

'Oh, and by the way, she was going to buy a mountain-bike for Joseph but she passed over before his birthday arrived."

This example of a good spirit message, broken down into its constituent parts, clearly shows the kind of standard to which all mediums should aspire. To finish this section, let's now see the complete link in its state of excellence:

An Example of an Excellent Spirit Message

'I have an elderly white-haired lady here with me: her name is Gladys Phillips and she was 78 years old when she died at home of a massive heart-attack. She tells me that her daughter found her body at the foot of the stairs, next to the kitchen door.

'She says her daughter's here tonight, and that her name is Janet Simpson. I'm told you're sitting in the front row of the gallery.' (Then point to the correct person and say:) *'Please speak up Mrs Simpson: I have a message from your mother tonight.'*

(The link is placed.)

'Your daughter's concerned about you, and about her family. She says she has three young sons, all boys, and they're missing her terribly. She wants you to tell them she's still alive, and that she cares for them deeply. She sends her love to them: their names are Michael, John and Joseph. The youngest one, Joseph, is particularly grieving for her. Tell him that she's fine in the Other World.

'She visits them all each day, including their father, whose name is Albert. Please send her love to the whole family.

'She also knows that you went to the doctor's last Tuesday (because she went with you) and he prescribed a course of blood-pressure tablets for you. She says, "You've been skipping two of them each day, and you're not following your doctor's orders to rest in the afternoon. Keep taking the tablets, Mum!"

'Oh, and by the way, she was going to buy a mountain-bike for Joseph but she passed over before his birthday arrived.'

Make Statements – Don't Ask Questions

This point cannot be emphasised strongly enough: a medium who stands before the public in order to prove survival of the soul after death should make statements of fact – he shouldn't ask questions. It's a poorly developed medium, indeed, who has to ask his recipients for the information!

Here's an excellent piece of advice for all mediums:

The only place where you should 'fish' for information is in the spirit world itself.

Eliciting Responses

You must allow recipients to respond to each fact that you supply. Don't roller-coaster along denying them the opportunity to say 'Yes', 'No' or 'I don't understand'. You're offering evidence of survival, and the witnesses (and you, yourself) need to know if the details are being accepted or refused.

But in eliciting a response, it isn't permissible to ask your recipients questions such as:

Has your mother passed over? Do you like to drink lager? Are you taking your children on a daytrip this week? Have you got a bad leg? Did your father work on the railway? Have you got a brother living in the USA? etc

None of these questions constitutes a mediumistic link, or a even a psychic link because *nothing has been stated*. This low standard of work should never be delivered in public anywhere in the world (but sadly, it often is).

To elicit responses from your recipients it is permissible to ask only questions such as:

Do you understand this message, please? Would you speak up, please? Does this make sense to you, please? Is this correct? Is this information significant, please? etc.

Mediums should state facts; their messages should not be vague and full of interrogation, and they should contain as much detail as possible. Keep on working at it, because the deeper your sensitivity becomes, the more accurate your messages will be.

17

Psychological Barriers that Affect a Sensitive's Work

Everyone wants to be accepted and respected, and when sensitives work in public this psychological desire is particularly evident. When the power is flowing freely and the messages are successful you feel comfortable and have nothing to worry about.

But when things go wrong, psychological barriers can rise in your mind and these can become powerful 'blocking-points' which, if unchecked, can stop your work completely.

How Psychics and Mediums Should Deal with Refusals

If the spirit information you're receiving is correct, deliver it confidently to your recipient; but if he refuses the information: *don't panic*! Smile, and remain calm.

Feelings of humiliation are born of fear: fear of rejection; fear of appearing silly; fear of not living up to your audience's expectations; and the fear of damaging your reputation.

But don't be afraid.

Remain calm, and exercise your maturity.

It isn't the end of the world. Everyone hits a bad

patch now and then. Handle the situation with dignity and cheerfulness, and always be ready with a sensible reply, such as:

- *You disagree? One moment please, and I'll try to clarify this further.*
- *Which details don't you understand, please?*
- *I'll check with my communicator and see if I can get more information for you.*
- *Please forgive me, but I think (your father; your sister; your brother;) is right. Perhaps an older family member will verify these facts when you get home.*

The important point to remember is this: *keep going*! If you take long and ponderous pauses, this can allow your emotions to cloud your aura and quickly 'block out' clear reception of your spirit inspirers' thoughts; the spirit people's minds work on quick and subtle thought-frequencies.

To prepare yourself to face refusals, do some homework on your platform presentation: write down ten different ways of dealing with refusals, then commit them to memory and you won't be stuck for words if things go wrong. Remember that some of the best evidence of survival is often refused at the time of its transmission; but if you're sure you're right, be steadfast.

To highlight this point, here's a signed affidavit from a Mrs Johnstone, taken from my book *Visions of Another World*:

Stephen O'Brien told me he was talking to my 'two uncles in spirit, both brothers,' and he named them as 'Uncle John and Uncle George'.

I strongly disagreed, telling him that I only had one uncle there, namely Uncle John. But Mr O'Brien stuck to his guns.

'There are two uncles,' he said. 'Ask and you'll find I'm right.'

So I did ask my mother, and to my astonishment the facts proved correct. My Uncle George had died before I was born and I had no knowledge of him whatsoever.

This message impressed me because it contained evidence which could not possibly have been read from my mind.

How can information that is not present in my memory be gleaned from it?

The only fitting explanation was that my two deceased uncles were speaking to the medium.

How Healers Should Deal With Power-Refusals

Healers can do nothing when cantankerous or cynical patients reject the power of the spirit. Patients can accept or refuse anyone's spiritual healing energies: they have freewill, and that is their prerogative.

To help the power to be readily accepted, and before the energies are delivered, healers should explain how they will administer the treatment quite naturally, which can allay any deep-seated fears their patients might have.

It's the healer's responsibility to create the right emotional and mental conditions (calmness and trust) in his patient's mind, after which the treatment is more likely to be successful.

171

'Bridging' when Paranormal Information is Slow to Arrive

When mediums and psychics are working, if the lines of communication are 'sluggish' and they've been unable to quicken them, they should use the skill of Bridging. Bridging involves linking two pieces of information with a piece of educational knowledge or another appropriate teaching-point, which will help to keep the verbal commentary in full flow. For example, if you receive a mediumistic link like this:

'There's a child with me, who's just passed over, (pause, pause, pause, pause). *His name is Thomas,* (pause, pause, pause, pause...) *And flowers have just been placed on his grave.'*

Too many pauses like this can bore your witnesses, which can cause you anxiety, and your work could then stop completely.

Instead of silence, fill in the gaps by Bridging them with educational information, which serves two purposes: it keeps the commentary and the spirit-power flowing, and it delivers a comforting message to everyone in the audience.

With Bridging applied, the above link might sound something like this:

'There's a child with me, who's just passed over. (Of course, all children survive death and will grow to maturity on the Other Side of Life, no matter how they pass over.) *I'm told this child's name is Thomas;* (and he's trying his best to link his thoughts with my mind to impress me with more

information, which, I think, is something to do with his resting-place. Yes), *flowers have just been placed on Thomas's grave.'*

This second version of the link is more interesting to listen to, and with the Bridging applied it will help new witnesses to understand something of the fate of children who die, and to realise how spirit messages are received.

Caution: *Your Bridging statements must contain only universally-recognised facts.*

You should possess a wide range of knowledge if you intend to disseminate spiritual truths.

(For example, one ignorant 'medium' was heard to 'bridge' that 'Sadly, we don't have any bodies in the spirit world, so we'd better hug all of our loved ones here on Earth, while we can!' This, of course, is pure ignorance: spirit bodies occupy space and are solid in their own dimension.)

Developing your Platform Style

Newcomers to public work sometimes copy the style of a famous personality whom they admire, but you should develop your own platform manner and delivery.

Be yourself. Even if you succeed in copying a famous sensitive's delivery, you'll only ever be second best to the original.

The preparation of spirit messages is not your responsibility (that task rests with the spirit people), but you *are* responsible for their delivery. You should present them with dignity, intelligence and compassion, and with a little well-placed humour (but only when appropriate, of course).

When you walk onto a platform you carry all your presentation techniques on with you, inside your mind; and you should use them to vary the style of your delivery as much as possible.

Exercises for Mediums to Improve their Presentation Techniques

You can improve your public presentation by writing down ten different ways of dealing with all kinds of difficult situations. For example, if you're about to describe an accident victim to his mother, you could begin the link in several different ways, such as:

- *I sense a tragedy here, and accident victim is with me...*
- *I have with me a young man who died quite tragically in an accident...*
- *I'm looking for a mother among us tonight, whose son died in a tragic accident...*
- *I can see a young man standing close by, and I feel he passed in a tragic accident... etc.*

Do some homework to improve your presentation techniques; using the above idea you can now expand on it. Write down, and then commit to memory, ten different ways of:

- *Starting a message.*
- *Placing a message.*
- *Encouraging an audience member to speak up.*
- *Describing a passing.*
- *Speaking about a child's passing.*
- *Speaking about an animal's passing.*

- *Speaking about a mother's/father's/husband's/ wife's passing.*
- *Announcing good news.*
- *Delivering a gentle reprimand.*
- *Delivering some responsible, universally-safe advice (such as, 'If you don't feel well, visit your doctor').*
- *Getting yourself out of a communications-breakdown situation.*
- *Dealing with a heckler (and hopefully not too often).*
- *Sorting out a crossed-link effect (two messages intermingling at once) and explaining to the audience what has happened.*
- *Expressing the love of the spirit people for their loved ones left on the Earth.*
- *Ending a message by expressing your thanks.*
- *Leaving a recipient and moving on to start a new message.*

Never be accused of boring your audience.

18

Speaking in Public

'When Should I Go Public?'
When the spirit people think you're ready to face
the world and bear witness to their existence in a
responsible manner, they'll certainly let you know;
but you shouldn't make this important decision
alone: consult with your helpers and your tutor.

You'd be wise to curb your enthusiasm and stop
yourself from jumping onto the nearest platform
before you're ready to serve with dignity, intelligence and reliability.

From behind the scenes, many spirit guides
'engineer' their mediums' first public appearances,
and the sensitives are often quite surprised to find
themselves unexpectedly working before a crowd
of people!

It isn't within the scope of this book to cover the
many aspects of public speaking, but anyone who
is about to step into the public arena might wish to
consider the following points:

Dress Code
When you work in public you're representing the
world of spirit and the organisation that has

booked your services.

You owe it to the public to be scrupulously clean and well dressed for the occasion. Pay particular attention to personal hygiene and to the colours you wear: a pleasant, clean appearance with all of your clothes colour-matched is pleasing to the eye. Don't wear several garish colours that clash.

If you're a man, dress plainly and try to project a clean-cut image; if you're a woman, avoid too many frills and flounces – and both sexes would be wise to choose one dominant, pleasant colour.

Wash and style your hair; clean and shape your fingernails, polish your shoes; clean your teeth and brush your tongue. If you're to stand under theatre spotlights consider applying a little make-up: powerful arc lights rob your skin of natural colour and give it a ghastly, ghostly hue.

The first impression the public receive about you is your appearance, and if you can't be bothered to show them respect by dressing well, why should they be bothered to listen to you?

And here's an extra tip for the ladies: wearing long skirts or full-length evening dresses is often preferable to wearing the shorter styles: in some theatres if you wear a knee-length skirt the people in the front row might see more than they paid for.

Projecting your Voice

Most theatres, halls, churches, and conference centres today provide microphones to amplify your voice, but in some places this technology isn't available and you'll have to project your voice – and this doesn't mean you must shout.

Shouting damages the voice.

The voice is supported by the breath, and you're advised to study specialist books on the Culture of the Voice, because its production and projection is an art form in itself.

Meanwhile, here are a few safe exercises to help you project your voice quite naturally.

Voice Exercise One
To bring sound of the voice forward onto the lips:
Keeping your throat and the surrounding region absolutely relaxed and tension-free, close your mouth and relax your lips, allowing the cutting-edges of your front teeth to meet quite naturally (some people may have to drop their jaws slightly to achieve this).

Now breathe in, just a little more deeply than you would normally. Keeping your mouth, lips and jaw tension-free, make a comfortable humming sound, and 'bring it forward' until you can feel your lips vibrating against each other and your teeth buzzing with the sound.

Keep the sound steady and of an even pressure – and there should be no tension anywhere; keep the throat particularly relaxed.

In all voice exercises remember this instruction: *Be as lazy as a cat in your throat and shoulder regions.*

Voice Exercise Two
To project the sound forward and out:
Prepare yourself as in the previous exercise, then, keeping your throat, jaw, and shoulders perfectly relaxed, hum your favourite melody.

Halfway through the tune, open your mouth and

gently sing each note of the song to the sound of 'Pah'. (The 'explosive' sound of the 'p' should help you to bring the sound forward and out.)

Repeat this exercise several times, using different sounds each time: Mah, Bah, Tah, Lah, Fah, Kah, Gah, Hah, Quah etc.

Daily relaxed singing or soft humming will help you to modulate the sound of your voice; that is, to move its sound up and down in the scale quite naturally.

Delivering a Public Talk or a Philosophical Address

This is another specialist subject that you should study, for its complexities are outside the scope of this book – but here are some helpful tips:

- Speak proper English (Learn its grammar and sentence construction).
- Speak clearly: enunciate your words (study elocution, breath control, and correct voice production).
- Modulate your voice so that it's interesting to listen to.
- Every talk should have a Theme, an underlying message that unifies the whole address.
- Every talk should have a beginning, a middle, and an end – and a point!
- Think about this old saying: 'First I tells them what I'm going to tell them; then I tells them; then I tells them what I've already told them.' (Get your point across clearly and unambiguously.)
- If you speak from personal experience, your talk

180

will resonate with sincerity.

- Never speak on subjects about which you are ignorant.
- Your talk should be educational: decide what information you wish to impart before the event (unless you're an inspirational speaker, of course, in which case this task must be left to your spirit world inspirers).
- Add some well-chosen, well-placed humour to lighten the experience; and do try to smile when appropriate!
- Don't go on and on repeating yourself: know when to stop. This advice was once given to a long-winded speaker: 'Stand up; speak up; and then shut up.'
- And the best advice of all: 'If you don't strike oil in the first two minutes – quit boring!'

19

Publicity Mediumship
Working with Hundreds of People

Demonstrating clairvoyance to the public in theatres and city halls is much more difficult than delivering it in Spiritualist churches or psychic societies: to command and then hold the attention of 2,000 people requires advanced presentation skills, which include projecting your personality to completely involve everyone at the meeting.

In large crowds, unless you get your facts absolutely right and hold the public's attention, they'll get up and walk out.

Before meetings begin, if you can hear the crowd is lively and chattering that's a good sign because they're 'awake' and are already communicating – with one another.

Conversely, a reverent, dignified quietness can also be helpful, but not when people sit in abject silence either because they're depressed, or fearful, or so pious that they're too afraid to move. In these circumstances, the medium has his work cut out! Such audiences are sometimes crudely described by sensitives as being 'dead from the neck up'.

These folk must first be awakened and then be 'prepared' to participate in a vibrant, joyous three-way communication link; and this preparation technique is an art in itself.

Sensitives must create the right kind of psychic atmospheric conditions in which they can work successfully: they should calm people's fears and encourage them to relax; and then gain their undivided attention – these procedures gently clear away confusion and fear and replace them with confidence and trust, and then the Power of the Spirit can operate more freely.

Believe me when I say: if the public like you, this certainly helps your work to succeed. The mental and emotional states in mass audiences can either nullify or encourage a meeting's success.

If the public decide they dislike you, your work will be difficult; in this instance, immediately try to build up their interest and soul-empathy *before* you attempt to demonstrate your abilities. (This is why I talk to my large audiences for up to twenty minutes prior to any spirit messages being given.)

All mediums are helped by the vibrant psychic energies radiated by sympathetic people, and by an atmosphere of trust between themselves and their witnesses. Without these positive energies, no warm rapport exists, and the sensitive will have difficulty in engaging his listeners.

There's more to being a public personality than just standing in the spotlight.

Dealing with Bored Witnesses
Here's the rule:

If the audience is 'alive', you can sail along on the tide of energy they create; but if the audience is 'dead' – *you* must come 'alive'.

Be more interesting and more charming.

And if your recipients refuse to speak up: don't take long pauses – keep the whole demonstration flowing as best you can. Whatever you do, don't allow the meeting to 'go flat' or to slow down: always keep it gently moving along.

What part do our spirit guides play in working with us from the Other Side of Life? How do they attune to us and work with us; and how can we help them in these tasks?

Here are some revealing insights and important teachings on attunement, spirit power, and other related matters, given from the spirit world's point of view as expressed by my spirit guide in my book *In Touch with Eternity: Communion with Another World*:

The most difficult sensitives to reach are those who are just starting out on their development: they haven't yet established the ideal mental and emotional states of peace and balance which we require to obtain and hold a close rapport with them. These mental conditions are essential for successful attunement to occur. That is what psychic and spiritual development circles are for: to learn self-control and the stilling of turbulent forces which so badly affect our links with you on Earth.

Mediumship means attunement.

When successful attunement takes place, communication flows. When attunement is out-of-focus the receiver (the medium) does not register us clearly. It is easier for us to reach mediums when they are cheerful, bright, optimistic, calm and mentally tranquil and also positively expecting success. But any fears or worries, anxieties and doubts — all of which create mentally-paralysing negative forces — and our clear links with them are seriously hindered. This is why sittings are unsuccessful in the presence of hostile minds. Those who wish to scientifically test the existence of us in Spirit must first look to their hearts before their intellect, their text-books, or their own stony beliefs. Open-mindedness and sincere kindness are essential ingredients for successful communication to occur.

But let us now move on...

Seen by us, the meeting-place is of little importance and its walls do not entomb us as they do you; we can pass through them because we vibrate at much higher rates than the physical atoms of the bricks. What we are conscious of is a vibrant pulsating electromagnetic light, a vast battery of life-power upon which we may draw and with which we must successfully blend in order to gain good attunement.

Around the immediate area of contact a large band of helpers in my world is carefully gathering and assessing all the electrical, mental and emotional conditions, and is also speaking to people who will try to communicate later.

But, although eager to relay their messages, communicators are not allowed to storm the medium: everyone is directed and organised and chaos is not permitted within the photosphere of sensitivity. We wait for attunement to take place at the meeting-point, but if our medium does not desire our closeness and refuses it, or is unable to raise his mind-vibrations to approximate our frequencies, then we are powerless – and our influence will be largely unregistered.

Now a few words about what occurs on Our Side during a public meeting.

Firstly, it is known to us beforehand who will be in attendance. We have access to a complicated network of interlinked thoughts and information, which can be tapped to discover who is likely to be present at the event. Though not an infallible system, it is very reliable, for everyone intending to come will have carried these thoughts in their minds for some time, and they are registered by trained people on Our Side. If, however, one of our projected recipients is *not* going to attend, then other spirit communicators are chosen and their relatives and friends on Earth are checked to see if they will be present. So one link replaces the other.

Ours is a very organised world: the power of thought is the quickest means of communication and, because of this, everything can be monitored faster than lightning-speed. We do not just gather on Earth and hope for the best, there is a great deal of unseen order and activity behind working mediums. There are many souls on our side who lend their valuable services towards the success of a demonstration. It is not a haphazard spur-of-the-moment happening, but is usually a well-planned and precisely actioned event, even though it can seem to be 'chaotic'.

Neither are the messages off-the-cuff haphazard affairs, they are usually quite well prepared. Communicators have been thoroughly counselled and reminded: 'Your loved ones in the audience cannot see, sense or hear you, but you must try to prove your survival. What can you say; what memories can you bring; what evidence could you give, or facts could you convey which would undoubtedly establish your presence?' They are also carefully advised to concentrate at the time of their transmissions and not to mentally 'wander away' or 'stutter' incoherently — though some do just that, being emotionally overwhelmed at the moment of contact.

In the early days of our association I stood very close to my medium and acted as what we term a Control. It was my function to tune my mind so precisely with his that we almost became one individual. Communicators then expressed their thoughts to me, which were instantly registered by him. In the initial stages of a medium's development, while he is still learning to build his own sensitivity, very often he does not work directly with communicators but rather with spirit controls. These are highly trained experts in communication who take overall charge of the medium and his work.

There are also others present who monitor his health and vital physical systems while the mediumship is functioning. But once a medium's abilities are strengthened and well established the controls step aside and the sensitive then works directly with the communicators on a positive mind-to-mind link. That is why people have sometimes remarked about Stephen's messages, 'It's just as though the spirit people are standing beside you. You make them very real.' To which he has often replied, 'They *are* very real.'

Because we are human beings and are not automatons or machines, communication sometimes falters, breaks down or appears to fail.

It is then my task to direct Stephen back onto the right track. I will often 'step in' mentally and say: 'You have made a mistake,' or 'Go back over it.' I have even had to tell him, 'Your recipient is lying,' when one man refused evidence which we knew to be true.

My medium hears far more from us than ever he expresses, and that is because thought is lightning-fast, many thoughts are conveyed in the time it takes to physically vocalise one word.

Our mental links are sometimes so subtle and tenuous that it comes as no surprise when our connections to the medium suddenly break. There is then hurried activity here to do all in our power to re-establish contact as quickly as possible.

Because Stephen's abilities are now reasonably established (there is always greater unfoldment ahead, and no medium for the spirit world is ever fully developed), he works directly with communicators and often hears their voices as they were on Earth.

Sometimes their language is none too polite! This, we believe, adds to the authenticity of the messages because he is often amused by what he hears and therefore he spontaneously laughs. He is also sometimes emotionally moved by the deep poignant sadness as certain communicators remember their last moments on Earth, and this often makes audiences realise that what is taking place is indeed a very real process.

All good mediums are sensitive beings: it has to be so, or they could not be channels for the subtle and refined forces of the Spirit.

Those who don the mantle of service as prophets, seers, visionaries and mediums must expect their emotions and thoughts to become more acutely heightened. It has to be so; a human receiving and transmitting station — or medium — can only be in touch with eternity when the psychic faculties are sharply, finely tuned.

And once our co-operators have discovered and unfolded their innate soul sensitivities they cannot ever lose them: they remain operational for ever. This is why we advise all mediums to cultivate tremendous self-discipline and a willpower of iron, and to master control of the self: a medium should always be in full charge of his abilities, and not vice-versa.

It is the medium who 'tunes in' to our world (where we are waiting) — and the medium who 'tunes out' of our wavelengths.

We are not dictators, and you are not puppets dancing on our strings. It is always a conscious and willing co-operation between us, for our work is founded upon a mutual link of love, trust and service — not on domination.

Behind Stephen, as he works, there can be upwards of eighty spirit helpers surrounding him at large public meetings. But there are also countless other spirits who come to witness demonstrations, too. They know they are not going to get a chance to communicate but nevertheless they remain in the vicinity to observe the powers at work. Occasionally they move unseen amongst audiences and perhaps stand by their special loved ones, trying to convey the thought of their presence and continued care and concern. This has prompted some of the public to say, 'Although I didn't get a message from the medium, I felt my people were there.'

The joining of Two Worlds can be an emotional, soul-stirring experience and it is not uncommon for people in both planes to weep when messages are being relayed. Their souls are touched. But of course there is also much laughter, too, especially when comical memories are transmitted, or when things go wrong.

Sometimes when two or three communicators are waiting near the sphere of sensitivity and one of them is unsuccessful — or recipients are unwelcoming — a new communicator will jump his turn and transmit a brand new link and, of course, Stephen receives it. This is a 'crossed-line' effect, when two messages are coming in at once. Not all spirit people are well-mannered. After all, they are human beings under emotional pressure and we have to make allowances. But through all this confusion Stephen must remain calm at its centre, and try to sort it out. Sometimes he has to start the link again until the lines are cleared.

There have been times when we fully knew, even before we tried, that messages would go unclaimed by audience members. There are many different reasons for this, which I believe Stephen has written of, but the main one is *fear*. Thoughts of public humiliation or embarrassment also make recipients unwilling to participate. In Stephen's case all these fears are groundless, for he conducts himself with dignity in public; but the audiences' fears make our work so very much harder than it already is.

After transmission, communicators often weep at the realisation of their success in getting, perhaps, only a few words through to those who love them; or if their links have been refused; or if they have not quite been accurately attuned and Stephen has not heard or sensed them properly.

It is regarded as an experiment by my world, too; but communicators are not left comfortless. We take them aside, congratulate them, console them and speak about the joy they have added to the evening's events and to their loved ones' lives.

When Stephen is inspired to conclude the meeting, which often lasts two and a half hours, applause rings out in the theatre and we know our service has been appreciated.

But we are not always certain at this time just how much of what we have transmitted has actually been received by him and delivered to the audience.

This is because we are concentrating on our medium as well as focusing on communicators and energy levels. (There are even doctors monitoring Stephen's heartbeat to ensure he is not over-strained or anxious. If he is, then they step closer and calm him by the power of their thoughts and inspire him to slow down and not to rush. There is a great deal of hidden activity out of physical sight.)

Afterwards there is usually a celebration on our side, a raising of joyous voices which makes every effort worthwhile, during which we have the inevitable dissection of the evening: not only by the communicators but also by our experts here.

We are learning all the time.

We then leave Stephen's orbit and go our separate ways. We are not always beside him: spirit controls gather to perform specific functions and then depart until the next call to service.

No one with you has the power to demand or

command us to do his bidding; and we are governed by the same laws here: we cannot make anyone on Earth accept our teachings or our inspiration.

Freewill is a Universal Law.

. After service, mediums often notice their personal power-reserves have been drawn upon; and this is so. All mediums utilise their own energies when working with us. The physicist's definition of work is any activity which burns or expends energy. That is correct. In a medium's case the main loss of energy dissipates through the physical nervous system.

But the more power the audience gives, the less of the medium's own energies are utilised. All public demonstrators feel slightly tired after services simply because a great deal of power is burned up in their trying to convey meanings succinctly, as well as in physically conducting the meeting.

It is very stressful to stand before a thousand people with nothing in your head except utter trust in the voice of the spirit, and a prayer that we will maintain our mental connections with you and prove our presence to the listeners.

The communications are 'live'; there is no script or rehearsal, it is all spontaneous; and it either spontaneously succeeds or fails. But we will not fail you.

It is my custom to remain close to Stephen for a short while after working, to inspire him to rest and get plenty of sound sleep, pure water, good food and clean air, for these are the constituents which build up the physical body and replenish the nervous system. I also impart some of my own power reserves to help him in these processes. His spirit will never tire, for the spirit is for ever linked to the eternal source of life, the Great Spirit — God — though the mind can sometimes become quite weary and in need of some tranquillity and a change of surroundings.

The great tasks upon which we in the Spirit are engaged, this work of spreading knowledge of an eternal life and all the deeper implications it brings in its wake, call upon all the physical, mental, emotional and spiritual resources of the human instrument.

We feel extremely grateful and privileged whenever we link with mediums who have dedicated their lives to helping us preach the good news: *There is no death. You cannot die. You are as immortal as Consciousness Itself.*

To all Servants of the Spirit I say: never be downhearted or allow doubts to assail you about your magnificent efforts to spiritualise and enlighten mankind. You are representatives of the greatest power in the Universe — the Great Spirit of Life. You are His Ambassadors, carriers of the Living Light of the Spirit, a light that will ever guide you and never falter. Neither will it ever be extinguished.

We are here in your world to stay.

We need no church, no special creeds, no certain race or person — but we will work with all those whose hearts are pure and whose minds are fixed upon helping mankind towards the discovery of eternal spirit truths.

Go forward then with love in your hearts and with the desire to help all those who stand in spiritual darkness and ignorance of the truth, and we will step with you. We will not forsake you, or leave you comfortless.

We are your friends and we love you.

We are attracted to you by the goodness and compassion in your hearts.

There is still much work for us to do: the harvest is plenty but the labourers are few. But if you will only co-operate with us, together we can change the world.

*

Stephen, could you tell us more about what it feels like for you when you're working as a medium? And could you speak about the psychic energies you use?

There are three teachers which every sensitive ought to acknowledge: Perspiration, Hard Work, and Experience.

At meetings in which the psychic and auric audience conditions are good, I sometimes start receiving messages in my dressing-room before I take the stage; but on 'poor' nights when energies are low, in my earlier days I'd have quite a struggle to establish my first contact.

But at most demonstrations these days, I begin receiving messages only when I've taken the stage and am just about to launch into my links.

Most times, like other mediums, I have to 'kick-start' my psychic abilities into action, which is rather like starting a car engine on an icy morning; then there's a warm-up period while I tune-in more precisely to the spirit link and get into my stride.

When working mediumistically, several soul-abilities might function at once. In my own case, I usually see, sense, and hear my communicators with varying degrees of clarity. However, down the years, I've developed my clairaudient abilities because hearing communicators' voices means I'm able to deliver more accurate factual evidence.

The spirit voices are sometimes quite objective (almost sounding physical), but their strength and quality varies according to both my communicator's and my own ability to accurately tune-into our respective mind-frequencies.

The psychic atmosphere generated by the crowd also adversely effects or positively helps me to succeed.

Many spirit voices sound quite faint, manifesting merely as a thought-voice within my mind.

However, with good contacts I'm even able to discern regional accents.

Often two or three voices might clamour for my attention: and if a link goes unaccepted or the voices are confused, it's not uncommon for a new communicator to suddenly burst in on the message and try his luck, which can create a muddle of voices, which can be confusing or amusing.

Some spirit people are so desperate to communicate their survival that they forget their manners, and every possible expletive that's ever been used on Earth, I've also heard from the Kingdom of Heaven!

How do you see your spirit communicators?
The spirit people make direct contact with me on the platform. I often see them standing near me,

sometimes clearer than I can see the audience in front of me, and at other times simply as a flash of an image.

On occasions the communicators stand near their people in the auditorium; however, they tend to appear wherever the greatest amount of power gathers, which might not be in the same area as their recipient.

In my early days, this caused me confusion and sometimes I linked my communicators with the wrong recipients. This mistake can still be made now, though thankfully rather more infrequently!

20

Service

Have you any good advice for mediums who are struggling to learn their craft?
Yes: be patient, and never be discouraged.

Carry on; and always do the best you can.

Remember that each service you perform is unique: psychic conditions will vary, audience responses will vary; the quality of your thoughts and health will vary; and the amount of detail you're able to receive will fluctuate. Sometimes communication-lines are faint, and at other times they're stronger and more reliable.

Remember that mediumship is an experiment, which can – and sometimes does – go wrong.

Don't be overly-critical of your abilities; you're not a puppet or a computer – you're a fallible human being.

But don't give up.

Persevere; and you'll reach your goal in the end.

Remember that you've promised God and the spirit world that you will serve – do so, then, as best you can. No one can do better than his best.

Don't be drawn into the fantasy that every great medium of the past always gave brilliant displays of psychic power, and that they always produced marvellous results. Know that they, too, had their difficult services, just as you will have.

But you should continually strive to improve your skills and to unfold your spiritual progression.

And here's some good advice about your future:

Once you develop your mediumship or psychic powers what are you going to do with them? You can only give them away in service to others.

True spiritual service is about educating people, comforting, and healing people.

Service is about helping the human race to spiritually awaken and progress; it's about being a living example of what it is to be a compassionate soul: it isn't about fame or fortune.

Those who single-mindedly seek fame and fortune might well achieve it for a short time, but the real treasures are of the spirit: loving, serving, dispensing comfort, helping people out of the darkness and into the light, offering sensible guidance, educating, and giving hope and healing.

These are the everlasting spiritual treasures that can never be lost.

I wish you great success in your work; and even though I can confidently predict that the road you'll tread won't be an easy one, if you're meant to walk it – walk it you will.

And my love and good thoughts will go with you.

May God guide you well; and may your spirits soar.

PART TWO

Everyone Can Heal

*More on Unfolding your
Natural Healing Powers*

Important Notes from the Author

Although this section contains specific instructions on how to further unfold your natural healing powers, all of the teachings in Part One of this book, on the development of psychic and mediumistic skills, are relevant to the healer's pathway.

Therefore, I advise healers to read this book in its entirety, for each section contains vital information that all sensitives should know: the teachings encompass the development of many aspects of soul-sensitivity and soul-awareness, from which all branches of your spiritual life and work may benefit.

Healers would be unwise to study only this section.

All readers should find material to interest them in the following pages because they contain important information on how to attain good health.

*

***WARNING and DISCLAIMER:** If you possess an unbalanced emotional or mental nature you should avoid developing mediumship or any form of psychic skill because the spirit power-processes involved in this development can excite your nervous system and agitate your thought-patterns. It can also affect the delicate balance of your body's hormonal systems and its endocrine (or ductless gland) structures.*

If you have received any form of psychiatric or psychological treatment, or have undergone clinical depression or any other form of mental or emotional illness, which includes drug abuse or alcohol addiction, then do not proceed with any form of psychic or mediumistic development without first seeking approval from your doctors.

Developing your soul-abilities can affect your entire physical, mental, emotional and psychic being, and it is a very serious undertaking – it isn't a light-hearted 'pastime' or a toy to be played with for idle amusement.

The Hippocratic Oath
A Modern Version
(Hippocrates, a Greek Physician: 460 - 377 BCE)

Although many historians agree that these words weren't written by Hippocrates, today's medical students still take this oath upon graduating.

I swear in the presence of the Almighty and before my family, my teachers and my peers, that according to my ability and judgement I will keep this Oath and Stipulation.

To consider all who have taught me this art equally dear to me as my parents, and in the same spirit and dedication to impart a knowledge of the art of medicine to others. I will continue with diligence to keep abreast of advances in medicine. I will treat without exception all who seek my ministrations, so long as the treatment of others is not compromised thereby; and I will seek the counsel of particularly skilled physicians where indicated for the benefit of my patient.

I will follow that method of treatment which, according to my ability and judgement, I consider for the benefit of my patient, and will abstain from whatever is harmful or mischievous. I will neither prescribe nor administer a lethal dose of medicine to any patient, even if asked, nor shall I counsel any such thing: I shall show the utmost respect for every human life, from fertilisation to natural death, and shall reject the act of abortion that deliberately takes a unique human life.

In purity, holiness and beneficence, I will live my life and practice my art.

Except for the prudent correction of an imminent danger, I will neither treat any patient nor carry out any research on any human being without the valid informed consent of the subject or the appropriate legal protector thereof, understanding that research must have as its purpose the furtherance of the health of that individual.

Into whatever patient setting I enter, I will go for the benefit of the sick and will abstain from every voluntary act of mischief or corruption and, further, from the seduction of any patient.

In connection with my professional practice, or not in connection with it, whatever I may see or hear in the lives of my patients which ought not be spoken abroad, I will not divulge, recognising that all such information should be kept secret.

While I continue to keep this Oath unviolated, may it be granted to me to enjoy life and the practice of the art and science of medicine with the blessing of the Almighty and the respect of my peers and society; but should I trespass and violate this Oath, may the reverse be my lot.

21

Preparation of Body, Mind and Spirit

Could anyone learn to heal?
Yes; love is the motivating power behind all acts of healing.

Spiritual healing is a form of mediumship that can best be developed under the guidance of reputable healing mediums, whom you may contact in your own area.

To further unfold your natural healing abilities, join a reputable recognised organisation, such as the ones operated in Britain by the Spiritualists' National Union, the Greater World Christian Spiritualist Association, or the National Federation of Spiritual Healers etc. Search the Internet for addresses of other renowned societies in your own country.

Read as much good literature and teaching material on the healing arts as possible. The late and renowned healer, Harry Edwards, wrote a number of informative and thought-provoking volumes about spiritual healing, many of which are still in print (see *Recommended Reading*.)

Will my great love for people make me a great spiritual healer?

Your capacity to express unconditional love will mark you out as a great soul, but you will become a great spiritual healer only when you add to this love a well-developed mediumistic attunement with the spirit world.

Basic Anatomy

Every responsible healer should, at the very least, make a basic study of the human body. There are many fine books available, and you don't need to go too deeply into the subject: a basic knowledge of the main organs and the bodily systems will serve you well, particularly when patients share with you what's wrong with them.

However, you shouldn't pry into your patients' personal details: this information is given either voluntarily, or not at all. And don't forget that the spirit people already know what your patients' problems are.

Preparing to Become a
Good Healing Channel

Healers, especially, should be as healthy as possible in body, mind and spirit in order for the purest and highest forms of spiritual healing energy-rays to be transmitted through them to those who are suffering in the world.

That's the ideal; but many practitioners fall short of these high standards.

A healer's patient once said to me, 'My healer smokes and drinks alcohol, but he's a wonderful channel and he produces marvellous results.' My reply to her was, 'He'd be an even better channel if he aligned himself with the laws of health.'

On deeper esoteric levels, healers should be aware that 'dead' meat contains toxins from the slaughtered creature's system, as well as body-hormones (meant to be consumed only by its offspring), and often chemicals, and, of course, the psychically-impregnated memory of its horrific death, which remains powerfully impressed within every cell of the meat. This negative psychic energy remains alive in the tissues, and it can later become programmed into the spiritual blueprint of anyone who consumes it.

Here are some words of wisdom on this subject, conveyed to me by spirit beings, and taken from my book *The Spiritual Keys to the Kingdom*:

Resolve never again to harm another being, which includes those souls in the animal kingdom.

From today onwards stop eating meat and generate within you a greater respect for The Spirit of God which resides within your sentient brethren in the animal kingdom, who are still so cruelly abused by the spiritually ignorant.

In order to spiritually progress, you must change: you must increase your ability to be compassionate, and you must respect the planet upon which you live.

Does your love reach out beyond the scope of yourself and your immediate family? Here is one way to check if it does:

Are you kind to animals?

Don't eat meat – don't buy it or cook it for anyone else.

Do you think God's Angels are pleased when a callous being terminates a life?

You cannot create Life, therefore you have no

right to take it.

These are thought-provoking statements.

And for the same psychic reasons already stated, no compassionate healer would wear animal fur.

Becoming a Vegetarian or a Vegan

If you decide to adopt either of these cleaner lifestyles, you should read as much good literature as possible so that your daily intake of proteins, vitamins and minerals is sufficient to maintain health. Contact the Vegetarian or Vegan Societies in your own country, and they will advise you how to proceed safely.

Vegetarians and vegans need to pay particular attention to their intake of B-complex vitamins, for a lack of these can lead to nervous exhaustion and poor health in the nervous system.

It's easy to become an irresponsible vegetarian (someone who doesn't eat meat or fish) and it's even easier to become an irresponsible vegan (someone who doesn't consume or use animal produce of any kind, including milk and dairy products), and to damage your health.

Obesity, Anorexia, and Bulimia

Try to keep your body healthy and to reach the ideal body-weight for your height, build and age. Gluttony and obesity often indicate an emotionally imbalanced personality; morbidly obese people aren't well-balanced and healthy human beings, and neither are bulimia sufferers or painfully thin anorexic persons.

Obesity, bulimia and anorexia are often caused

by emotional or psychological conditions. If you're suffering from one of these complaints, or you have a personality disorder, you shouldn't develop your healing abilities until you've eradicated the cause of your problem. Consult your doctor and an enlightened nutritionist, and receive professional life-counselling (ask for Cognitive Behavioural Therapy).

Coupled with a great deal of willpower, good counselling can often restore sound health.

But the Scottish materialisation medium, Helen Duncan, was a remarkable channel for the spirit world; and she was a very large lady, wasn't she? Indeed she was. Mrs Duncan weighed twenty-two stone (308 lbs), and her excess of fatty-tissue and blood plasma were used by her spirit guides to create amazing fully-formed temporary physical bodies in which spirit communicators manifested.

Helen Duncan was a remarkable deep-trance medium, and she was special in all senses of the word.

She was also the exception that proves the rule.

I'm stating the ideals that we should try to follow.

Smoking, Drug and Alcohol Abuse, and Other Addictive Habits

The health warning is clear: smoking kills, and it also harms others in the vicinity – so don't do it.

Smokers aren't healthy people: they're tobacco addicts.

And on a note of personal hygiene, smokers' clothes smell dreadful and so does their breath and their fingers. Their homes and sanctuaries often reek of tobacco, and this is hardly an advertisement for a healthy lifestyle.

I applaud the health-poster of a man's face wearing a gas-mask, underneath which is written: *No Smoking, please: people are breathing.*

Other unhealthy addictions include the abuse of drugs or alcohol, which can damage your physical health and dull your psychic senses.

Exercise moderation in all things.

Can the Sick be Used as Healing Channels?

The answer is yes: spiritual healing energies can pass through the healer's physical and psychic bodies even if he's unwell; though the most effective treatments are usually delivered through the healthiest practitioners.

A healer acts somewhat like a copper wire that carries electricity from one point to another.

If a person is incapacitated or confined to a wheelchair, this doesn't mean he can't be used as a healing channel; there could be many reasons why someone is ill in this lifetime, including karmic ones (more on this later).

A life of service may be an important part of a sick person's reason for incarnating.

Any sincere motive to serve others with a compassionate heart will draw the assistance of compassionate people in the spirit world.

Like attracts like.

Spirit healing doctors and chemists will use any means at their disposal to fulfil their mission of healing the world and its creatures.

In cases like this, the healer's motive is the most important factor.

Lifestyle Choices for Improving your Healing Abilities

What kind of character traits do you think a true healer might possess?
Genuine spiritual healers are gentle, loving people with compassionate and kindly natures.

They're usually sympathetic and empathetic souls whose personalities soothe and comfort people in distress: they nurse the sick, offer friendship to the lonely, and give solace to the suffering and the grieving. All true healers are patient and tolerant individuals who are dedicated to rendering service to others.

Could you sum up for us what kind of broad lifestyle a spiritual healer should follow?
The most effective healers are those who try to live cleaner, healthier lifestyles and who cleanse their bodies and minds of as many impurities and negative energies as possible.

Kind thoughts for others and a tolerant, non-judgemental attitude are essential qualities needed by any compassionate spiritual healer.

The more balanced the healer is (physically, mentally, emotionally, and spiritually), the greater will be the amount of the God-Power that can flow through him.

Some Do's and Don'ts of a Healing Lifestyle

- *Don't eat or drink excessively.*
- *Don't smoke, or pollute your system with unnecessary drugs.*

213

- *Don't eat meat.*
- *Don't overtax yourself, or allow stress to affect your health.*
- *Don't think you're a 'special' messianic or saviour-like figure: you're not.*
- *Don't harbour unkind thoughts in your heart against any person or any creature.*
- *Don't be cruel, vindictive, or jealous towards others, and don't isolate yourself from society.*
- *Don't allow people or difficult situations to upset your inner tranquillity.*
- *Don't assume that the spirit world will teach you everything you need to know: they won't.*

- *Do eat well and wisely, and ensure that your bowel-movements are regular.*
- *Do drink plenty of pure water, and breathe clean air.*
- *Do keep fit and healthy, and take some regular exercise, but find time each day to rest your mind and body.*
- *Do sleep well.*
- *Do meditate daily.*
- *Do be compassionate and serve others with a willing and loving heart.*
- *Do read up on your subject and study it thoroughly.*
- *Do remember that you are not the healer, you're only the channel: acknowledge the Supreme Power, God, the Great Spirit.*

To increase your health and your personal battery of healing energy, re-read the list on *Basic Healthy Tips to Increase your Store of Personal Psychic Power* in Part One of this book.

22

The Body's Natural Healing Powers

The body, mind and soul, which are all powered by
the Life-Force or the Spirit of God, have a natural
tendency to heal themselves. If you cut your skin,
without any conscious effort on your part your
body's natural defences will immediately try to
repair the damage; and this happens because your
spirit is programmed to survive.

Cell Intelligence
Every cell of the body has its own intelligence: each
cell thinks for itself, and the healer's task is to help
the patient to create within himself the ideal
conditions that will allow this intelligence to heal
his body, mind and spirit.

The healer's tasks are to:

♦ Convey healing energies to the sufferer's spirit,
  which will then try to balance, re-align, or
  revitalise the patient's energy-fields, which in
  turn will try to heal the patient's body.

♦ Help the patient to understand, and then to put
  into practice, the basic laws of physical, mental,
  emotional, and spiritual health.

Poor Nutrition, a Lack of Exercise, and Personal Responsibility for Health

Every day, billions of people are digging their graves with their teeth.

A vast majority of disease stems from poor nutrition and a lack of movement. If people followed the advice of enlightened nutritionists, a majority of their health problems would correct themselves in quite a short time.

We are what we eat.

Billions of people fail to provide their bodies (minds and spirits) with the natural proteins, minerals and vitamins, amino acids (and many other essential spiritual, mental and emotional ingredients), which would keep them in tip-top condition. I speak of 'enlightened' nutritionists because I don't believe that eating animal flesh is a good basis upon which health should be founded, but many nutritionists do.

Other healthier forms of protein are available to us in this modern world, and we should make use of them.

Good nutrition is essential to good health, and healers should point this out to their patients. They should also educate their patients about the Law of Personal Responsibility. We are each personally responsible for attaining, and then for rigorously maintaining, our state of health.

Karmic Illnesses

Do you think we suffer from some illnesses as a result of our Karma? Do we experience the pain that we ourselves attract into our lives through Karma, the Universal Law of Cause and Effect?

Yes, this is possible. We can draw to ourselves all forms of physical, mental, emotional, and psychic dis-ease through the hidden karmic forces at work within us – no matter how unpalatable this idea seems. If we accept we've lived many lifetimes, the mathematical operation of the Law of *Cause and Effect* could explain why seemingly blameless and innocent individuals are now experiencing all manner of hardships or disabilities.

This issue is worthy of serious debate.

How can I free myself of my Karma?

If you know you've wronged another being in this life, or in any previous lives, your debts are usually repaid by rendering service to them. I believe we can't begin to experience true spiritual freedom until we resolve these conflicts, one by one.

Many opportunities to set the record straight will present themselves to us in this lifetime because the Law of Karma compels us to associate with members of our own soul-group, who are living either here on the Earth, or in the Beyond. Family circles, old friendships, spiritual, social and religious societies, past enemies and people with whom we've shared unpleasant experiences – all these forces will attract us in this lifetime because we've either been associated with them in past lives, or we've spent time with them in the spirit spheres during our sleep-life.

Man is continuously evolving his spiritual nature by facing and resolving the multifarious challenges of the heart and mind that he attracts to himself through the Law of Karma.

And the ultimate prise for all this effort is a closer

Union with God, which brings a blessed sense of peace and freedom to the spirit.

Could a healer's karmic debts affect the amount of spiritual healing energy he can transmit?
The answer is yes.

Just go forward and serve others to the best of your ability. No one could ask any more of you.

Success Rates, and The Limitation of the Power
No healer can guarantee that a treatment will be successful, or that it will effect a cure.

Your success rate will vary according to the many conditions that govern the work: your health, the patient's health, the karmic health conditions of your patients, the psychic and spiritual conditions in and around the healing-room, all of these factors can affect the results. Most healings occur gradually, not instantaneously – though this is, of course, possible. Many small miracles have taken place and these are well documented.

Healers can never guarantee a cure, or even that a condition will be alleviated: the best they can do is to tell the patient that there are no limitations on the power of healing. The rest is up to God, if the patient is religious; or to Fate, if he is not.

When Healing Fails
Why do some patients fail to respond to spiritual healing, and pass over?
When it's time for a person to make his transition, nothing will prevent his going; though it's true to say that spiritual healing can ease his pain and

help him to leave the Earth in a more peaceful frame of mind, and with greater dignity.

There's a time to be born; a time to live; and a time to die.

There's a time for everything – even for pain and suffering.

Many respected spirit guides teach that we can receive only what we've earned for ourselves, which could help to explain why some people fail to respond to any form of treatment.

Patients themselves can also reject or thwart the healing power, as can the karmic forces within them.

Sometimes healers end up battling against the odds. For instance, if you treat a woman who can't breathe properly and then she smokes a cigarette, the healing can only be a palliative measure. In order to regain full health she must first give up her addiction to tobacco.

Remember, too that healing 'fails' when hypochondriacs possess their illnesses and nurse them as treasured possessions, and refuse to let them go.

But even if a cure isn't effected through a healer, the patient's mind and soul can still be touched by the spiritual experience.

The Power of Hope
A great part of a healer's work is to offer hope to people who've given up on ever regaining health or peace of mind. It's a sad fact that many patients turn to healers of all descriptions only as a last resort, which is why Hope is such a powerful medicine.

Dispense hope regularly, but don't forecast a

cure: that is beyond your jurisdiction. However, you can, and should, be optimistic and show your patients that someone cares about them, both in this world and in the next.

Your patients will place their trust in you, and therefore you have a great responsibility to ensure that this trust is never broken or betrayed.

Unconditional Service

It isn't the healers task to convert his patients to his own belief-system. Healers shouldn't offer their services on the condition that their patients first receive religious instruction, of whatever sort.

Spiritual healing should be offered because it's needed, and compassion should motivate your work. Don't emulate the dreadful example of offering homeless people a bowl of soul only *after* subjecting them to your own theology.

This is a morally abhorrent practice, and healers should play no part in it.

23

Magnetic Healers
and Spiritual Healers

What is a spiritual healer?
A spiritual healing medium is a person whose
finely-attuned psychic abilities allow him to
channel spirit energies from the Source of All
Power – God – into the spirits of those suffering
from any form of disharmony or dis-ease.

What is a magnetic healer?
A magnetic healer is a person who projects his own
energies into the psychic atmosphere surrounding
his patients, without the aid or co-operation of
discarnate helpers.

The German physician, Franz Anton Mesmer
(1734–1815) who devised the system known as
mesmerism, which is recognised today as the
forerunner of hypnotism, believed that there was
an occult force or an invisible fluid emanating
from his body. He claimed that this same kind of
energy permeated the Universe, and he later
developed the practice of passing his hands over
his patients' bodies (in what we now recognise as
the auric field) and thereby transmitting his own
magnetic power to them.

221

Magnetic healers use this system of magnetic passes today.

How can I tell if I'm spiritual healer or a magnetic healer?

After delivering treatments, magnetic healers can sometimes feel tired or drained of their vitality because they've transmitted some of their personal energies to their patients.

Conversely, spiritual healing mediums don't feel nervously depleted after working because they co-operate with discarnate specialists to convey spiritual energies to the sufferer – just as copper wires conduct an electrical current.

Spiritual healers often feel more relaxed and refreshed after delivering treatments because the spirit people often leave some of their own healing power with them.

Are patients who receive magnetic healing from me exposed to any danger?

Yes. It's possible for a magnetic healer to boost a patient's store of psychic energy, which in turn could be absorbed by a growing tumour.

Magnetic healers should take great care when choosing whom they help.

People suffering from physical exhaustion or nervous debility usually benefit from a magnetic healer's energy-boost, but the kind of character-ised, corrective energies which can effectively treat or cure diseases are more likely to be delivered through a competent spiritual healing medium.

Why have I been gifted to manipulate the bones of

my clients, whose arthritic conditions have vastly improved?

Healing is an ability that everyone possesses, but few people develop it to a remarkable degree. If I were you I'd think twice about using any form of manipulation, acupressure or massage on your patients (unless you're qualified in these skills) because if you aggravate their conditions, they could prosecute you for assault upon their persons.

For this reason, healers ought to be accompanied by a chaperone whenever possible. All reputable healing organisations issue Codes of Practice and Guidelines to their members about these topics, and you'd be wise to follow them.

You don't need to touch a patient, of course, to administer spiritual healing energies, which I will discuss in more detail shortly.

Trance Healers
Do healers need to be in trance to transmit the most effective healing rays?

No; but when spiritual healers are working proficiently – that is to say, when their minds are properly attuned to their spirit helpers – they sometimes experience a gentle shift of awareness or an 'overshadowing'.

However, in this modern world, deep-trance healing is an anachronism and many spirit guides have cast it aside in favour of a more natural association.

A deep-trance state can also be disconcerting to witness, particularly if a man's personality overshadows a woman's and she speaks in a deep voice while she stomps around the room.

These days, this kind of practice is unnecessary.

Try to be as natural as possible, and remain fully awake while your powers are in operation.

Does my guide 'take over' my body, or 'step inside me' when we give healing to others?
No. The spirit people bring about all forms of mediumistic control through a close association with their medium's mind and aura. Guides don't 'get inside' their mediums' bodies; not even the medium is 'inside' his own body – he's closely associated with it.

Physical Sensations When Healing
Why do my hands feel hot or cold when I'm healing?
These are just reactions to spiritual and psychic energies, which may vary greatly throughout your period of service. Some healers feel 'pins and needles' or experience the sweeping sensations of an electric energy – but don't worry about these.

Healing can take place even when you think nothing unusual is happening.

And do resist the temptation to grimace or distort your features while working: this kind of dramatic exhibitionism is quite unnecessary.

Spirit-Healing Guides and Doctors
Will I always work with the same band of spirit healing guides?
No. New controls will arrive as your sensitivity deepens, but some of your closest helpers will probably remain with you throughout your period of service.

A number of healing-controls were once doctors, surgeons or pharmacists and suchlike when they lived on the Earth, and they'll continue their work through someone like you from the Other Side of Life.

Healing Diagnosis
Should I diagnose illnesses?
No; you're a spiritual healer, not a doctor.

Many patients often feel emotionally vulnerable, particularly if they've sought your help after the medical profession has given up all hope of them making a recovery, and the last thing they need is a dubious psychic diagnosis.

In Britain, it's illegal to diagnose unless you're a qualified doctor or veterinary surgeon. But why would you need to, anyway?

Your spirit friends can clearly see your patient's health reflected in his aura, and they'll do their best to treat his ailments.

Should I tell a patient he's going to pass over, if my spirit friends confirm this?
No – definitely not.

Such a staggering thought could psychologically disturb or deeply depress your patient.

You'd be wise to deliver your treatment and keep your thoughts to yourself.

Should I tell my patients about the clairvoyant messages my guide wants me to give them while we're administering healing?
No; and if I were you I'd ask my spirit guide to concentrate on the healing process rather than on

relaying survival evidence. Neither of you should give clairvoyance during a treatment because these two abilities operate on different psychic wave-lengths.

If necessary, survival evidence can be given after the healing session.

My healing group leader ticked me off for giving psychic counselling while delivering healing. Was she wrong to discourage me?
Unless you're a professional counsellor – and the training to qualify can take several years – then don't attempt to give advice to anyone, at any time, because your ignorance could cause your patients serious psychological damage. (Re-read the section on the dangers of counselling in Part One of this book.)

Obsession, and Mental Illness
Is it possible for someone on Earth to be obsessed or possessed by a spirit entity?
Before answering this question, let's take a look at why the idea of possession is still prevalent today. Here's a story taken from the King James Version of the Bible; Luke, Chapter 8, verses 26-35:

And they arrived at the country of the Gadarenes, which is over against Galilee.

And when he went forth to land, there met him out of the city a certain man, which had devils (a) long time, and ware (sic) no clothes, neither abode in any house, but in the tombs.

When he saw Jesus, he cried out, and fell down before him, and with a loud voice said, What have

226

I to do with thee, Jesus, thou Son of God most high? I beseech thee, torment me not.

(For he had commanded the unclean spirit to come out of the man. For oftentimes it had caught him: and he was kept bound with chains and in fetters; and he brake the bands, and was driven of the devil into the wilderness.)

And Jesus asked him, saying, What is thy name? And he said, Legion: because many devils were entered into him.

And they besought him that he would not command them to go out into the deep.

And there was there an (sic) herd of many swine feeding on the mountain: and they besought him that he would suffer them to enter into them. And he suffered them.

Then went the devils out of the man, and entered into the swine: and the herd ran violently down a steep place into the lake, and were choked.

When they that fed them saw what was done, they fled, and went and told it in the city and in the country.

Then they went out to see what was done; and came to Jesus, and found the man, out of whom the devils were departed, sitting at the feet of Jesus, clothed, and in his right mind: and they were afraid.

Let's examine this story.

First, we should remember that the Bible is a copy of a copy, of a copy, of a copy etc, and that over the centuries its texts have been so radically altered, embellished, and reinterpreted by many minds that we cannot be certain that the above events actually took place.

Indeed, some scholars now doubt if Jesus ever lived: they believe he might be a heroic allegorical 'Everyman' figure, woven about with miracles and legends, which presents Christians with a pattern of a moral and religious life that they should follow. There's certainly little historical evidence of his presence on Earth, if any, that is beyond question. (See *Recommended Reading*.)

But is there *any* truth in this story about Jesus and the 'possessed' man?

Let me state emphatically that no one in the spirit world can 'possess' anyone here on Earth. If this were possible, each night billions of us would leave our bodies fast sleep and travel into the spiritual worlds, and then we'd return in the morning to find someone else 'inside' them.

It doesn't happen, because possession cannot take place. Your body is uniquely yours.

However, *obsession* does occur, but this is quite a different matter.

At some time during their period of service, most healers will encounter patients who claim they're possessed by devils or evil spirits, and much of the blame for this misguided concept must be laid at the feet of the Christian Church, which, believe it or not, still performs distressing exorcisms on these poor souls today.

Most people, however, would agree that we can be obsessed by strongly-held ideas. 'Alexander the Great' was drunk with the concepts of absolute power, Empire-building, and the subjugation of other races, and at any cost. And it's well known that fanatics of all kinds are fascinated by their idols.

(To date, I've had seven different stalkers, all of whom were motivated by sexual frustration and loneliness; though none of them was aware of this fact).

Mental imbalance is more common than we'd like to think, but severe mental illness falls into a quite different category. The tortured souls who suffer from personality disorders, mental anguish, delusions and hallucinations, and who hear 'voices' in their heads that command them to self-harm or to kill others, or to cause havoc in other people's lives – all of these souls need our prayers and our compassionate healing energies, coupled with the tender loving care of their doctors and therapists.

Dealing with the Influence of 'Misguided' Spirits

I not happy with the word 'evil', I prefer the term 'misguided'; however, there is definitely 'evil' in the world.

There are many malicious, aggressive souls on Earth whose influence causes immense suffering and harm to humanity and to the animal kingdom.

The presence in all nations of terrorists, fanatical suicide-bombers, religious maniacs, murderers, rapists, criminals and tyrants verifies this fact.

If further evidence be needed you only have consider the daily murder of countless millions of animals, often in gruesome and horrendous ways, in and out of slaughterhouses, and you'll be left in no doubt that humanity still has a very long way to go before it can claim to be motivated by Love.

In the first part of this book I stated that everyone is influenced by spirit people of a like mind, and that the immutable law of *Like Attracts Like* is continuously in operation. Kind people attract kind souls, and cruel people attract souls filled with hatred or vengeance, etc.

But what about people with mentally-disordered minds? Could schizophrenics (split-personalities) attract mischievous personalities from the next world, who might try to confuse them or influence their thoughts and actions?

The sad answer is yes, this is possible.

We're all subject to the Universal Laws, which are no respecter of persons. Earthbound entities (that is to say, people whose materialistic passions and gross desires bind them close to the Earthworld and its vices, pleasures and pains) are everywhere.

Our good moral, mental, spiritual and emotional lifestyles 'push' these misguided souls away from us: spiritually and psychically, our minds and auras naturally repel people who aren't on our wavelength of existence.

When mentally or emotionally-ill patients are given medication to tranquillise their anxious minds, their quietened thoughts become de-sensitised to the presence of discarnate influences: that's how a part of the treatment works, though I doubt if many doctors understand this.

And here I'd like to emphasise that medication alone isn't the best way to treat mental illnesses. Psychological Life-counselling (also known as Cognitive Behavioural Therapy) should be given to correct the mind-patterns of these unfortunate patients, and medication should be gradually decreased until they become well again. But it's often a very long and hard road to recovery.

We alone hold the keys that open up the doors of our minds to the spirit people.

The possessed man in the Biblical story, if he existed, was behaving in a way psychiatrists would recognise, but very few of these would attribute this to 'demonic possession'.

We should remember that in the ancient world there was no powerful corrective medication, no diagnostic scanning equipment; there were no X-ray machines or any of the scientific advances we benefit from today. In the Old World, all kinds of distressing illnesses were attributed to 'devils' entering into people's minds.

The Law states that malevolent *dis*carnates are attracted to malevolent *in*carnates.

Keep your heart and mind pure, and you won't encounter these influences.

But mischievous entities abound on Earth and in Heaven and they can, and sometimes do, influence people's thoughts. The problem with mental illness is this: when the patient feels clinically depressed or mentally anxious his willpower weakens, and certain people in the spirit world might then take advantage of this. How then can a healer deal with removing mischievous entities from a patient's auric fields of sensitivity?

A four-pronged attack is advised. Healers should make certain that their patients are receiving:

1. **Medical Treatment:** tranquillisers and other treatments can often suppress hallucinations and remove the patients' feelings of deep anxiety, if only temporarily.
2. **Cognitive Behavioural Therapy:** should be

given to the patient (and often to his family and friends) by trained professionals.

3. **Contact or Absent Healing:** is delivered more effectively when the patient's mind is in a calm state.

4. **Spirit Intervention:** ask your band of spirit healers to remove any mischievous discarnates from the patient's auric sphere of sensation, and to offer him protection until he feels stable enough to regain normality.

Caution: If you're a magnetic healer, mentally ill people might have their conditions aggravated or excited by a power-boost from your personal energy-stores.

I wouldn't advise magnetic (or psychic) healers to deal with severely mentally- or emotionally-ill patients; a spiritual healer's services are to be preferred.

Spiritual healing can be given at any time, of course; but I believe more healers should make their patients' families aware that therapy should also be given to their loved ones.

Compassionate healers should also pray for help to be given to their patients' families, carers, and friends, because their needs are often overlooked.

24

Contact Healing
The Laying-on-of-Hands

How does the laying-on-of-hands work?
It isn't essential, of course, for the attuned healer
to touch his patient because spiritual healing
energies travel in the following way: they come
from the Great Spirit, *through* the spirit of the
healer, and *into* the spirit of the sufferer.

From there, these vibrations may redress any
imbalance within the individual's energy-fields,
and this re-harmonising or re-tuning effect can
help to restore health.

However, some patients feel neglected if you
don't touch the affected parts of their bodies; but
exercise caution here: it might be acceptable to
touch a man's chest, but not to touch a woman's.

You could ask the lady to place her own hands
over her chest and then you could rest yours over
these, if that's the way you to choose to heal.

Respect your patient's dignity, and remember
that clothing doesn't need to be removed. You're
dealing with energy-rays, not ointment.

With regard to where you might safely touch a
patient: holding his hands, while you're both
seated facing each other, or placing your hands
lightly on his shoulders while you're standing

behind him, is acceptable to most people.

Do I need to 'flick' my fingers or wash my hands after treating each person, to remove the negative psychic vibrations that seem to cling to them?
You can flick your fingers if you like, but this isn't necessary. However, you should always be clean and well presented, and it's common courtesy and a rule of hygiene that you should wash your hands before and after each treatment.

They say that cleanliness is next to godliness.

Healing via the Astral Cap and Spinal Cord
If the spirit people don't guide you where to place your hands, the afore-mentioned hand-positions will serve you adequately, but you could also send rays through the astral cap and the spinal cord.

Place one hand over the patient's crown chakra (on the top of his head, over what is known as 'the astral cap'), and place the other over the patient's solar-plexus chakra, which is found between the end of the breastbone and the navel.

With your hands in these two key-positions, the spirit power forms and adequate circuit of energy along the spinal column. But in any case, the power will flow to the affected body parts.

Some Legal Considerations
Should healers be insured in order to administer any form of healing?
I would advise it. Contact healers should obtain insurance cover, in case someone makes an allegation of misconduct against them and the case proceeds to court. For this reason, healers should

be chaperoned when they're working, especially if they intend to touch people. Some forward-thinking healers set up discreet digital or CCTV cameras to videotape their sessions.

Should healers advise patients about medication or medical treatments?
No. A healer should not, in any circumstances, override the authority of his patients' doctors: medical matters are the sole responsibility of the medical profession.

Is spiritual healing an alternative therapy or a complementary one?
Spiritual healing is a complementary therapy that should go hand-in-glove with medical treatment. It's also an alternative therapy, but it isn't meant to be an alternative to medical treatment.

Whenever they can, healers are advised to work *with* the medical profession.

Don't forget that there are many forms of healing, and doctors and surgeons are healers, too.

Should healers treat someone who declines to be seen by a doctor?
I'd advise against healers giving contact healing to anyone who refuses to seek medical aid; but you can pray for these people, of course, and help them in that way.

I know of one man who was diagnosed with cancer but refused medical treatment, preferring to receive spiritual healing.

His faith was great, and he experienced a wonderful sense of spiritual upliftment and peace, but he died shortly afterwards.

Massage and Joint Manipulation

Should healers practice the manipulation of joints and bones, and should they give their patients massage therapy?

As previously stated, these treatments should be given only if the healer is properly qualified to do so. In contact healing, and particularly when the healer manipulates or massages the patient's body, he can lay himself open to allegations of assault or of aggravating ailments.

Animal Healing

All of the above advice also applies to the healing of animals. Whenever you're asked to treat a sick or injured animal try to establish if it's been examined by a vet. Wherever possible, work in co-operation with the patient's veterinary surgeon.

Psychic Surgery

Is psychic surgery (physically opening-up and then re-sealing the skin) a necessary practice?

It's certainly a controversial one, which could lead to a nightmare litigation scenario.

I don't believe psychic surgery is necessary because while co-operating with well-developed healing mediums the spirit people have been known to dematerialise malignant tumours, and even to withdraw pieces of fractured bone from a patient, without puncturing the skin.

I think the need for this form of controversial 'surgery' is created within the mind of a patient who feels he can be cured only by being operated on. And where there's a demand, a supply is usually forthcoming.

Record-Keeping

Opinions are divided on whether or not healers should keep written records of their patients' visits. It's very much a personal choice, but if any legal problems arise, written records could prove invaluable.

If you do decide to write down people's personal details or store them on a computer, in Britain, under The Data Protection Act, you're legally obliged to protect this information. Seek advice from an IT advisor. And if you operate an absent healing service, in which your patients write to inform you of their progress, keep their letters secure under lock and key.

The Right to Confidentiality

Your patients' right to privacy and confidentiality should always be respected, and no healer should discuss his patients' private matters with anyone; except, of course, with another reputable healer from whom he may need advice or help, or with the police or the judiciary if legal proceedings are involved.

The Need for Faith

Does spiritual healing work on faithless animals and children?

Spiritual healing is a psychic science, and the patients who receive it don't need faith in order for it to work, and neither do they require any form of religious belief.

But a strong conviction that the treatment will work, certainly helps.

If a man believes he can be cured, a mental state known as the Placebo Effect comes into play, which can kick-start within his spirit a powerful self-healing process.

Scripture says the Nazarene asked his petitioners, 'Do you believe I can heal you?' And when they answered 'Yes', he's reported to have replied, 'Then your faith has made you whole,' or 'According to your faith be it unto you.'

These are thought-provoking statements, worthy of serious consideration.

To Charge or Not to Charge?

This is a matter of conscience and personal choice. (See my comments on fees, earlier in this book.)

But here's a cautionary true story. I heard of one healer who, with perfect trust in the guidance of his helpers in the Angel World, left his day-job and converted his bungalow into a sanctuary. He then worked full-time as a spiritual healer but didn't charge his patients fees. He didn't plan out or control his finances, his services were free and he relied exclusively on donations.

Unfortunately, six months later he was declared bankrupt and he lost his home.

If you do have to charge for treatments, what would be a reasonable consultation fee? I can't say: it's up to you.

However, you could work out what your total running costs would be for one year, and then divide this figure by 52, which will give you your required weekly wage.

25

Absent or Distant Healing
Healing by Prayer

How does absent or distant healing by the power of prayer work?
For any form of spiritual healing to work, a state of mental attunement between the medium and his spirit guides is necessary.

Thought is energy, and good thoughts (such as prayers) generate powerful, bright soul-lights in the healer's mind and auric energy-fields.

When praying for the improvement of a distant patient's health, the healer projects some of his own soul-energies towards the patient, and his spirit guides add to these a greater flow of power, which they then direct, by thought, towards the sufferer.

Will our prayers be heard?
Yes; every earnest prayer is heard by discarnate spirit listeners who exist on the same thought-frequency as the petitioner.

Although no genuine cry for help is ever ignored, the *effects* brought into being by the *causes* of a prayer aren't always to the petitioner's liking. What matters most is the loving quality of the Thought behind your invocation (i.e. your motivation) and the humble way in which you link with a much Greater Power than yourself.

Should we pray for ourselves, or only for the wellbeing of others?
You should pray for everyone, including yourself.

When praying exclusively for ourselves we are obviously being 'selfish'; however, if you see a downcast man on the street and ask for a healing blessing to be given to him, are you then praying for the man or for yourself, because you find his state upsetting?

Many prayers are not born of Love; they arise out of three powerful emotions: those of Fear, Greed, and Desire.

Countless people pray for guidance because deep within themselves they feel insecure, unworthy, or unloved; and they're often fearful of the future, or desperate to satisfy their dreams and wishes.

Relatively few prayers spring from the beneficent power of unconditional love, which is that rare kind of compassion that rises only from a truly selfless heart that seeks no personal reward.

Here's a sobering thought: in our present and quite limited state of spiritual awareness, we cannot ever know what would truly benefit another's soul – but we *can* discover the hidden motivation behind our own prayers.

Is prayer a necessary part of a spiritual life?
I would say, yes.

Religious people claim that prayer strengthens their faith and generates a great healing power, but others, who claim to have realised the immanence of God, believe that prayer is unnecessary because the Spirit of Consciousness is totally controlling the destiny every one of Its created life-forms, according to Its own Will, and therefore a mortal's prayer wouldn't change the Mind of God.

I find it difficult to pray to an impersonal, abstract Spirit; how does one pray to God?
God's Presence is within you. You already possess an intimate relationship with the Great Spirit. God is the Fount of Pure Consciousness from which you continuously draw your life-energy and awareness; therefore The Power is not only your Originator, but It is also your eternal Sustainer.

By turning your attention inwards, away from the gross vibrations of the physical world, you can more closely attune to the Essence of God within you, which is often experienced as a calmness enthroned in the deepest part of your soul.

When you're attuned or in a state of at-one-ment with the Divine Essence, you can draw power, guidance, inspiration, strength, and healing from the Source of Everything.

To help you reach this stage, here are some guidelines:

• Still your thoughts and relax your body; forget all your troubles and cares. (Closing your eyes may help you to relax).

• Once you've established within you a deep sense of tranquillity, speak your prayer either mentally or vocally. If you wish, you can direct your words towards some kind of vivid image

241

on which you can focus your attention; or you could think of a religious icon, or a candle-flame, or perhaps a picture of verdant peaceful countryside.

♦ Or you might feel more comfortable visualising God as a Great Light shining throughout your entire being, or only inside your head; or even radiating from the centre of your heart, where innumerable mystics believe God's Spirit is located within man.

Because the act of prayer is such an intensely personal soul-exercise, find the method that is best suited to your temperament and personality; but know that your prayer will be heard.

26

A Healing-Circle Prayer
delivered by Stephen O'Brien

Great Spirit of Life,
in humility we gather in this place
which has been sanctified by the power of love,
and we offer ourselves in service.

We pray that our minds will join with
compassionate souls in the Next World,
whose self-appointed task is to ease
the suffering of humanity,
and to heal the broken bodies, minds and spirits
of the human race, and of our brethren
in the animal kingdom.

Allow us, we pray,
to receive a Blessing of Healing Power
in this circle,
so that we may be used
to transmit its Beneficent Energies
to all those who stand in need of health
and revitalisation,
whoever they may be,
and wherever they may be;
we are all your Children.

With pure hearts and clean thoughts,
we send these requests
into The Great World of Light,
and we welcome now
into our midst
the Ambassadors of Health
and Wellbeing,
and the Angels of Love.

Bless this great healing work
with fruitfulness and success,
Great Spirit;
though we do understand that,
as in all things,
and at all times,
Thy Will
will be done...

*

A Millennium Prayer
for Peace throughout the World,
by Stephen O'Brien

May the Peace of the Great Spirit
touch our hearts and minds,
and the Souls of all those whom we love.

May people all over the world
think of Peace and Goodwill towards God's creatures.

May we find it in our hearts to forgive;
to heal; to make amends;
and to set ourselves at peace
with those we think have wronged us
in the past.

May we be Peacemakers...

May we give to our fellow-man
and to the animals in this world
the kindness which we ourselves would like to receive;
for we all stand in need of being healed,
and loved and respected –
and what we give out to others
will surely return to us in full measure...

And may God bless us and our loved ones with
The Peace that passes Understanding,
with The Spiritual Truth that will set us free,
and with The Light of Love that will heal all pain.

27

Sitting in a Healing Circle

Healers should sit in a weekly development circle, just as mediums and psychics should.

For instructions on the setting up of all kinds of circles, please refer to Part One of this book and read again the section on *Running a Successful Psychic Circle*.

Now let's take a look at some of the points that healers, particularly, need to consider when sitting for development.

Opening with Prayer
I would advise circle leaders to elevate the thoughts of their healers by beginning with a prayer: a spontaneous prayer should be spoken aloud by one member, and other prayers should be given mentally by each member of the circle. This practice will help to set the spiritual tone of the proceedings.

Entering the Silence
I shall repeat here what I've previously said about entering the silence (in Part One of this book).

Some healing groups play soft background music in the circle, and if this helps to instil a sense of calmness in the healers, all well and good; but it's better that they sit in absolute unbroken silence for at least half an hour, extending to one hour, once the circle has firmly established itself.

During the quiet time, the healers may learn how to discipline their minds, relax their bodies, and still their turbulent and anxious thoughts. Once they've established a state of inner tranquillity they're more likely to register the fine and subtle wavelengths of thought that are being radiated to them by their spirit guides.

During the silence, try to release the tension in your body, and try to quieten your mind.

Enter the silence and swim in its velvet embrace, and you'll soon discover that it's actually full of sound, both in the physical and especially in the esoteric (or inner) sense.

In no circumstances should this quietness be broken, not by incarnates or by discarnates.

Discipline should be upheld: anyone who speaks might disturb the delicate thought-patterns of his fellows. Discipline should be gently encouraged by the circle leader, who should also be the most experienced and intelligent healer in the group.

There will be plenty of time to speak, later on.

The Healing Book, and Sending the Power

Is any benefit derived from the weekly reading out of loved ones' names in our society's healing-book?

People on Earth may need this ceremony to obtain comfort and reassurance, but the spirit world (if it's doing its job properly) doesn't require this kind of repetition. Competent healing-controls can easily monitor the health of their patients because this can be seen in their auras.

However, following the silent time most circles choose a person to read from a healing book the names of the sick, asking that their conditions may be healed by the Great Spirit through His emissaries in the Beyond.

While this is being done, the rest of the group can either remain passive and quiet, or they can be active and send out their own magnetic healing energy-rays, or their absent or distant spiritual healing energies, to the people mentioned.

Caution: If you send out your own energies, then you're acting as a magnetic- or psychic-healer and you may experience a power-drain at the end of the circle. But if you're being used by the spirit people as a medium, then you're a spiritual healer and you should feel refreshed after the work is completed – provided that you wait a short while at the end of the circle, during which your guides will leave some of their power with you.

Could you provide us with some healing exercises, which we can do in our circle?
Yes, I can.

Exercise One, for Magnetic Healers
Encouraged by the circle leader, the healers visualise great rays of white light (which represent the God-Power) being attracted by their willpower down from the spiritual world and into their auric-fields.

Once the healers are filled with white light, they can then project it to all those who are suffering, wherever they may be.

If the patients on the healing list are known to you, you can hold in your mind a mental picture of them while your energies are being transmitted. This will help to focus the direction of the power.

Caution: *Be sensible, and don't exhaust your personal power-reserves during this exercise.*

Exercise Two, for Spiritual Healers

Once the healers have achieved a state of good attunement with their guides, they should then remain passive while the spirit-controls pass powerful healing rays through their auras and spirit bodies, and then transfer these rays to the spirits of distant sufferers.

You can help this process by breathing steadily and a little more deeply than you normally would; but take care not to make yourself dizzy by over-oxygenating your blood.

Using breath-power or the hidden cosmic force of *Prana* (or life-energy) in this way, may assist your efforts.

Exercise Three, for Healing the Earth and its People

All spiritual healers must learn to give.

Become still, and ask that the Great Spirit and His emissaries may use you to send out a vast golden, all-encompassing healing light to all the peoples of the Earth, and to all the animals, as well as to the members of the vegetable and mineral kingdoms.

Visualise the Earth turning majestically in space,

and through the power of your image-making mind enfold it in your golden light, or wrap a protective cloak of light and love all around it; or cup it in the palms of your giant hands and gently breathe your light of love onto all of its creatures.

Remember that 'the thought is the deed'.

Exercise Four,
for Recharging your Own Healing Batteries

End each gathering by revitalising your personal energies. The health of all healers is important not only to themselves but also to their spirit guides, who can work with them more efficiently if they're in tip-top condition.

Never neglect your own needs.

Before the circle closes, the leader should allow some time for each healer to top-up his personal psychic energy-store.

Draw down from the Cosmos a brilliant white, regenerating Light; then will it down through your crown chakra, and then allow it to flood your aura with radiance so that you become filled with light and power.

Both spiritual and magnetic healers may benefit from this psychic visualisation exercise.

Exercise Five, for Cleansing
the Healing-Room or Sanctuary

When the healers are relaxed and filled with white regenerating light, the circle leader can encourage them to pass their overabundance of light through the room, visualising it purifying and cleansing the psychic atmosphere of all negative influences, and replacing these with positive rays of peace and tranquillity.

Breathe in the light as if it were air, steadily, and then project the rays through the room as you breathe out.

After the room's been cleansed, the healers can then visualise it being filled with a calming blue healing-light.

This psychic exercise can have the same effect as when you spring-clean a well-used room in your house.

Exercise Six,
for Closing the Circle with Gratitude

All spiritual circles should close their proceedings by rendering thanks to the Great Spirit, and to their spirit helpers and friends for all the hard work, dedication, love and protection they give so freely – and for the care and compassion they've show to you, and to those who are suffering.

In a world whose people are becoming more and more stressed and self-centred, do try to set a shining example of good etiquette, and never forget to say 'Please' and 'Thank you'.

28

Colour-Healing

Is Colour healing (or Chromotherapy) a form of magnetic healing?
Yes, because it doesn't require the assistance of discarnate souls to deliver treatments.

Can anyone do it?
Yes.

How does it work?
Colour has a profound effect on our lives and also on our psychic and spiritual selves. You can use Chromotherapy to bring about healing effects in people and in animals but it's not a mediumistic skill, it's a psychic one. Colour-healing can be dispensed using tinted lights or colourful cloths, and no contact with the spirit world is necessary.

The cosmic properties of light and colour can penetrate man's psychic being to its deepest levels and can create harmonious vibrations within the spiritual matter that comprises his complex set of inner soul-bodies.

Colour-healing can also be accomplished quite effectively through visualisation. Through the power of his mind, a healer can project images of colourful rays, or of shafts of vibrant energy, to his patients.

But do take care, for, just as in magnetic healing, Chromotherapy might do the patient a disservice if the colours aren't chosen wisely.

Gloomy, drab and miserable hues can produce unsettling effects, but the brighter more positive shades can often encourage a sense of equilibrium and wellbeing.

To discover what kind of healing effects that colour and light might induce when either light-rays or coloured cloths are placed within the vibratory fields of a person's aura, here's a colour-healing list detailing the principal colour-shades and their possible psychic effects.

The Principal Colour-Shades (and their Possible Effects)

Red: stimulating
Orange: vitalising
Yellow: quickening
Green: harmonising
Blue: peace-inducing (pain-healing)
Indigo: purifying
Violet: silencing
White: regenerating

Other Popular Colours

Black: strengthening
Grey: neutralising
Rose-pink: soothing
Brown: stabilising

Are there any colour healing exercises we can do in or out of our circle?
Yes.

Colour-Healing Exercise One:
Create a Colour-Healing Room

If you paint your healing-sanctuary white, and then fix coloured lights along the walls or in the ceiling, you can illuminate it with the colours that you feel might help your individual patients.

Colour-Healing Exercise Two:
Using Colour to Heal Yourself

Keeping in mind the principles of Chromotherapy, why not redecorate your home, paying particular attention to the colours in your bedroom where you'll need the most peaceful hues because you'll spend one third of your life resting there, being 'bathed' in their healing properties.

Colour-Healing Exercise Three:
Experimentation

Discovering the effect that colours have on you:
You can test your depth of awareness and psychic sensitivity simply by changing the colours you normally wear.

If you wear a lot of black: try wearing white for a whole day.

How did you feel? What effect did this have on you?

Record your impressions, then over a period of days try wearing each of the rainbow colours to discover which ones make you feel comfortable and which ones make you feel ill at ease.

This experiment could reveal a great deal about your personality.

Important Note: *People wear the colours to which they feel most attracted, and in which they feel most comfortable, and they choose these colours because they're already dominant in their auric fields.*

Examples:
(Check the Chakra Illustration earlier in this book.)

1. *If a woman wears a lot of bright red on her torso, she's likely to be a positive, energetic and strong-minded individual.*
(The Heart and Solar-Plexus Chakras are strongly linked to emotion.)
A red hat might indicate that she has a willpower of steel.
If dark red is worn over the lower part of her torso, this could be a revealing statement.
(The Sacral Chakra, in the groin area, is concerned with sexual activity and procreation.)

2. *If a man wears a lot of pale blue on his torso, he's likely to be quite a spiritually-minded, peaceful soul who doesn't like acrimony or harassment.*
(The Heart and Solar-Plexus Chakras are linked to emotion.)
If he wears a dark blue hat, he's probably seeking to quieten his thoughts and bring greater peace to his mind.
(The Crown and Brow Chakras are concerned with Thoughts.)

29

Healing with Sound-Vibrations

When we hear the beautiful strains of a haunting melody, the mind is gratefully soothed and calmed, and the spirit is often lifted out of this mundane workaday world and into feelings of serenity.

Such is the power of music, when properly appreciated. And by music, I mean the timeless melodies created by Past Masters and not the often noisy modern-day rock or pop music.

Surrounding us, the great rhythm of Nature is like an orchestrated symphony, which contains such varied elements as dawn's peace and night's thunder, and the fresh sound of evening rain as well as the cheerful birdsong of morning.

We're constantly bathed by Nature's sound-vibrations, and the sounds in this pageant of Life are often mirrored in great musical works.

We may not be master composers but we can still appreciate and thankfully lose ourselves in the magnificent healing energies of their music. Down through the centuries wonderful music has moved and inspired us, and refreshed and healed our bruised and battered souls.

Music is a healing energy.

All musical notes consist of vibrations, and each sound is made up of its own specific frequencies or wavelengths.

So it is with our souls: we each have our own unique Auric Note or general key-sound, which is generated by our thought-patterns, feelings, and our underlying state of soul unfoldment.

Machines cannot yet register these high-frequency psychic or soul sounds, but sensitives have known of their existence for centuries.

Everything in existence is vibrating – even seemingly inanimate objects, which are no more than a mass of protons, neutrons and electrons constantly circling around so fast that they give the illusion of being solid matter. And every thing emits a unique auric or psychic note.

The Universe itself emits its own sound, as many Eastern religions have known for centuries, which sounds phonetically like the humming sound of AH-UM, and this became a mantra or chant-sound for several religious sects.

When we withdraw from the noise of the world and approach the golden chamber of silence, we can better attune ourselves to this music of the soul, to these vibrations of the Living Cosmos all around us.

In finding and blending with this inner musical sound we may become more conscious of our spiritual selves. We'll feel more at peace and At-One with the very Essence of our Being, which is the Great Spirit, out of which we all originated.

If ever you need to refresh, reinvigorate, or recharge your psychic being, you need only to rest in the peace of golden silence, and your body, mind and spirit can absorb the Universal Sound-Energies that exist all around it.

Even the chair you're sitting on is constantly sharing small energy-exchanges with you; and this principle of energy-transference is easy to understand.

In thunderstorms when two electrically-charged rainclouds come into close proximity, the higher-charged mass naturally sheds its power to the lower, which results in magnificent lightning. So too, when you become still, your body can actively absorb a power-boost from the environment: it can absorb energy from rustling green trees, rushing waterfalls, birdsong, radiant sunshine, clean air and pure water, and even from the walls of your house and the atoms of this book – all of these energies can boost your personal energy-store.

If you doubt this, when next you feel depressed: walk into a drably-painted dark brown-and-black room and see if these gloomy vibrations will raise your spirits!

Although natural psychic energy-interchanges are occurring all the time, we can absorb them more efficiently by an act of will, and anyone can do this: the Power is there for All.

You can draw more cosmic vitality towards you by stilling your mind, body and spirit, and then consciously allowing this soul-force to flow into you, around you, and through you.

To further increase your psychic energy intake (or to recharge your psychic healing batteries) during your quiet meditation-times, play some favourite classical music while allowing yourself to float into, and to be bathed by, its wonderful harmonies – and you will be doubly refreshed by its healing vibrations.

Try it, and see.

Life is about Motion, Vibration, Movement and Constant Change. Life is also like a musical score orchestrated by a Master Composer: somewhere He lives Unseen, yet strangely He is Ever-Present Within Everything.

But we should remember that great musical pieces nearly always have discordant notes in them: as well as waves of pure harmony, broadly linked to the main key signature, there are also sounds which momentarily disturb us – but they often resolve back into the original key, leaving us touched by beauty.

Life's like that: wonderful, but not without its jarring discordant times; yet these unsettling experiences help to make the Symphony of Living such a richly rewarding and valuable experience.

We're continually creating the Music of the Universe, and adding to it, day by day, our own unique auric sounds, which are manifested in our actions, thoughts and feelings.

Moment by moment, you are scoring each note of your life as it unfolds down the stream of time.

Some well-remembered souls lived their lives in a most gentle and thoughtful way, and lovingly shaped them with their kind actions.

They created a wonderfully healing and harmonious sound. To bask in the spiritual presence of these people is like being in Heaven itself: time stands still; the soul is touched, and it feels and loves without words.

What kind of song are *you* singing?

*

Healing-by-Sound Exercises

Healing-by-Sound, Exercise One
Use this exercise to establish in your mind and body a general calmness, which may encourage healing to take place.

Sit yourself, or your patient, comfortably on a chair (or lie down on a couch) and close your eyes while you play some soft, ambient, and relaxing background music.

Listen to the gentle tones of the music and allow the melody and its calming sounds to bathe your soul with peace and to quieten the thoughts in your mind.

You might fall asleep: if so, all the better – the exercise has relaxed you, and when you wake you'll feel refreshed.

Healing-by-Sound, Exercise Two
Use this exercise to help combat hypertension.

To help you to feel the sound-vibrations while you do this exercise, place the palm of your hand over your upper chest region, just below your collarbone.

Throughout this exercise you should keep your lips, jaw, throat and shoulder muscles in a state of relaxation (this isn't as easy as it sounds).

Choose a musical note that's way down in the scale of your voice (a note which, when you hum it, vibrates the resonant cavities deep within your chest) and hum this low note for about two minutes; taking breaths whenever necessary.

Try to keep the sound steady and of an even pressure; but don't get tense.

Caution: *when doing this exercise sit comfortably, or lie down, because the extra intake of oxygen might make you feel dizzy.*

If this happens, stop immediately, and resume the exercise when you feel more like your normal self.

Healing-by-Sound, Exercise Three

Use this exercise to help you combat a sense of listlessness or depression.

Sit yourself (or your patient) upright on a hard-backed chair and close your eyes.

To help you to feel the sound-vibrations while you do this exercise, rest the palm of your hand on the top of your head, over your crown chakra-point, so that your forearm is directly in front of your eyes; and relax...

Throughout this exercise you should keep your lips, jaw, throat and shoulder muscles in a state of relaxation.

Choose a high musical note which is at the top of the scale of your voice (a note which, when you hum it, vibrates the skull bones under your palm) and hum this note for about two minutes; taking breaths whenever necessary.

Try to keep the sound steady and of an even pressure; but don't get tense.

Caution: *when doing this exercise sit comfortably, or lie down, because the extra intake of oxygen might make you feel dizzy.*

If this happens, stop immediately, and resume the exercise when you feel more like your normal self.

30

Healing with Crystals

Is crystal-healing a spiritual healing power or is it a magnetic energy?
Crystal healing utilises the personal magnetic energy of the healer, but spiritual energies can also be transmitted through the healer and the crystals.

Can anyone do it?
Yes. Using gemstone crystals might help you to unfold your natural healing powers and encourage you to direct your energies directly to the places where they're most needed.

Crystals can be used to channel, conduct, or deliver a boost of psychic healing-energy either to those who are sick, or to yourself.

How does it work?
Millions of years ago, crystals were formed deep within the Earth from gases, rocks, and liquids being subjected to immense pressure.

The resulting psychic energy-waves that crystals now radiate can affect the vibrations of your inner spiritual body, which may then reflect these benefits upon your physical self.

Human beings (and animals) radiate their own

vibrating high-frequency energy-fields, known collectively as the Aura; and gemstones emit psychic vibrations, too, which can help to amplify and conduct your personal soul-energies to your patients.

The atoms of every thing in the physical world are in a constant state of movement – nothing is stationary or solid. Even the book you're holding is a mass of atomic particles circling around each other so fast that they give the illusion of being a solid object; but in reality, physical matter is an open network of vibrating energy-particles.

Using gemstones, you can help to harmonise the vibrations in your patients' auric-fields and spirit-bodies, which may then help to improve their state of wellbeing: spiritually, emotionally, mentally, and physically.

The colour of each crystal gemstone is a physical manifestation of the rate at which its matter is vibrating: the darker its colour, the lower its vibration – the lighter its colour, the higher its vibration.

You can choose which colour gemstones to purchase and use by referring to the Colour Healing List, printed earlier.

Caution: Doctors should always treat illnesses, of course, but crystals are quite safe to use as a Complementary Therapy at any time; and each time you use your crystals your own magnetic life-force or soul-power energises them, attunes them more closely to your vibrational fields, and boosts their power.

How to Use Gemstones
as Healing-Conductors

+ To effect a general spiritual vibratory tone-up or
  tune-up throughout the day, the easiest method
  is to simply carry any chosen crystals on your
  person. Turning the gemstones over in your
  hands can also generate a stress-relieving effect.
  When the gemstone feels warm it has attuned
  itself to your auric vibrations.
+ For longer-term benefit, crystals can be placed
  inside your pillowcase at night: but be cautious
  (!) the vibratory effect of some gemstones may
  excite your spiritual senses and disturb your
  sleep patterns. Always make considered choices.
+ Select the colour of the crystal to which you feel
  most attracted, then lie in a quiet semi-darkened
  room; relax and breathe deeply several times.
+ Place the gemstone on, or over, the specific areas
  of your body that you feel might benefit from its
  power, for about 10-15 minutes (any combina-
  tions of crystals can be used: see the Chakra
  Illustration in Part One).
+ Afterwards, breathe deeply several times, stretch
  your limbs, and ground yourself by going about
  your daily life as normal.

When using gemstones to amplify the transmission
of your personal magnetic healing energies, you
should relax your mind and try to visualise the
clouds of psychic life-energy which surround both
you and your patients, and then direct these
powers as you feel inspired.

Remember that 'The thought is the deed'.

Gemstone crystals may be used safely whenever

you feel the need.

You can deliver crystal healing energies in any way you please, but some of the following suggestions might prove helpful:

♦ Hold a crystal over any chakra-point and use your power of creative visualisation to imagine clouds of white or blue healing light (these are universally-accepted healing colours) gathering around your body, and then passing down your arm, through your hand and out through the crystal into the chakra energy-vortice you've chosen. Making gentle clockwise circles with the crystal might help you to concentrate and deliver your soul-energies more efficiently.

♦ Gently lay the crystal on any affected part of the body, place your hands over it, and then visualise and direct the healing light to your hands and to the gemstone, as described above. (*Remember that whenever you treat a patient, you should respect his sacred space and his dignity.*)

♦ While delivering the healing light, as described above, gently move the crystal horizontally or vertically along any affected parts of the body in small brush-like movements or in larger sweeping strokes, as you feel inspired. Propel the crystal through the spiritual/auric energy-fields surrounding the patient's body, directly over his or her clothes, in a series of magnetic passes.

♦ Sit quietly in a meditative and prayerful attitude with the crystal resting in your hands, which should be placed on your lap. Relax your mind and body. Breathe deeply several times until you feel peaceful within. Link up to God, the Great Healing Spirit, and, as you send out your healing prayers, the crystal may help you to focus the psychic power that you wish transmit to those who are sick or suffering.

31

The True Purpose of Spiritual Healing

What is the ultimate purpose of spiritual healing?
Strangely enough, the true objective of spiritual
healing is not to physically heal the patient (this a
fortunate by-product), but rather to help him
realise that he has a living and eternal link with his
Divine Creator which can never be broken; that he
is a part of the Everlasting Divine Parent which
created him; that he is a spiritual being who will
live for ever.

From this knowledge comes a wealth of mind-
opening thoughts, and the patient may then begin
to realise his spiritual potential, and understand
the reasons why he was born. These realisations
may then herald further spiritual revelations.

Spiritual healing should touch and awaken the
soul of man, and should make him aware not only
of his origin, but also of his destiny.

Spiritual healing should help mankind to realise
that because the Spirit of God is in Everything,
every man, woman, child, and animal on the Earth
is a child of the Same Divine Parent – therefore,
we are all brothers and sisters.

When humanity realises this great truth, perhaps
peace will establish itself on this troubled planet.

PART THREE

Powerful Spiritual Laws and Ethics,
and
Understanding the God-Power Within You

Important Notes from the Author

The importance of this section, and of the next (*The Power of your Mind and Thought*) might not at first be appreciated by some readers, but if you're about to open the doors of your mind to potentially billions of souls in the world of spirit, the quality and character of your thoughts will draw to you only those of a like mentality. Sensitives with lazy or narrow-minded thought-processes are unlikely to attract the wisdom and guidance of advanced spiritual beings.

During your period of service, the public will ask you many questions. People will seek you out and will quite happily bestow upon you an aura of knowledge, which you'd be wise to actually possess. The public expect sensitives to offer them intelligent guidance; therefore, ignorance should find no place within your mind.

As we increase our knowledge and life-experience, wisdom gradually builds up within us, increasing day by day; no responsible sensitive can work to his full potential if he remains ignorant of some of the basic universal laws and spiritual ethics, and the workings of the mind, all of which information he will need in order to advance along the path of spiritual progression.

In the rest of this book, I'll present some challenging thoughts, some basic philosophical questions, and some significant spiritual ethics. If you're new to philosophy, don't feel anxious: *philosophy* simply translates as *a love of wisdom*, and anyone who's ever asked himself questions such as, 'Does God exist?' or 'Is my life predestined, or do I have Freewill?' is already a philosopher.

If some of my thoughts contradict your beliefs, welcome this openly, for no one has ever progressed without first re-examining his mind.

My advice to all readers is: don't skip these later sections of the book; their purpose is to exercise your mind, and they might raise more questions than they answer.

Powerful Spiritual Laws
and Ethics

32

The Hand of Fate?

Do you believe in coincidence?

Do you believe there are such things as accidents; or do you think your life has been planned for you?

Has your existence been predestined, unalterably mapped out for you before your birth? If your answer is 'yes', then who did this planning? Was it you, or was it some other intelligence?

Or perhaps you think life is simply a sequence of random, haphazard events?

What do you believe?

Are you governed by Fate, or do you operate within the confines of a bestowed Freewill? And if you do – who bestowed this Freewill upon you? And when was this gift given?

Such philosophical questions as these have tested the minds of great thinkers down through the centuries, and they continue to make us reassess our belief structures today.

Over many years as a medium, numerous spirit communicators have told me of the circumstances surrounding their deaths, and because of these experiences I've come to believe that each one of us is meant to die at a specific time.

Furthermore, I believe that until we reach that

time, our transition cannot be taken.

I believe our births are pre-ordained, too.

On my widespread travels, and also through my postbag, I've met many troubled people who tried to commit suicide without success, and others whose medical prognosis of surviving a serious illness was nil – yet none of these people died; they remained on Earth.

On occasions, terminally ill patients who had no hope of any improvement went on to make complete recoveries and outlived their medically predicted passing-dates sometimes by several years.

This is why I believe that whether taken quickly, slowly, tragically or with dignity, a passing is made only when the time is right; and so great is this conviction that I concluded my autobiography, *Visions of Another World,* with this philosophical statement:

'And when we look back upon our experiences in Earth-life, we will notice how all the things we did, happened in just the right places, at just the right times. And we shall say to ourselves – it is good.'

To back my claims, here's a true story related to me by a matron of a busy city hospital, and it concerns two cardiac-arrest patients.

One heart-attack victim was a young and healthy athletic man in his early twenties, and the other was an elderly woman in her late eighties.

When their hearts arrested they were both given immediate resuscitation, but, quite astonishingly, the young man died, and the old woman lived.

Their consultants were more than perplexed by this because the life expectancy of the old woman had been nil, whereas the young man's medical prognosis had been excellent – yet it was he who passed over, and she who survived the trauma.

Furthermore, a post-mortem was conducted on the young man and no real cause for his failure to respond to treatment was found.

It's obvious to me that the young man's time to die had arrived, and the old lady's soul had more work to complete on Earth before she could pass over to the Other Side of Life.

More intriguing stories spring to mind, and one involves a report made in the 1960s by an infant girl from Aberfan, the village in Wales where a whole generation of schoolchildren was killed by a moving coal-tip.

On that fateful day when a mountain of black mud slid down the hillside and smothered nearly all of her classmates, the little girl point-blankly refused to go to school.

Earlier that morning she had thrown tantrums and had argued vehemently with her mother – behaving quite unlike her normal self – yet because of her passionate desire to stay at home, she lived to tell the tale.

Was her life spared simply by a matter of Chance, or did her soul know of the impending tragedy?

Could it be that some part of her Higher Self realised that she wasn't yet destined to die?

My answer to these questions is *yes*; but you must draw your own conclusions.

This next account was told to me by one of my mother's friends, whose son had been called up for service in the Second World War. When he set off to join his ship he arrived seconds too late and missed it: his taxi was delayed, and he was forced to take the next ship out.

Later, the ship he should have sailed on – the one he narrowly missed – was attacked by the enemy and sunk, with nearly all hands lost.

What had really happened on that day?

Had the unseen Hand of Fate mysteriously touched his life and quietly guided his, and other peoples', actions to bring about a purpose?

Or had his life been spared simply by Chance?

Some people might say these stories are simply examples of coincidence in operation, but in a well-ordered Universe, in which Universal Laws rule Supreme and for every *effect* there is an underlying *cause*, there doesn't seem to be much room for chance.

Indeed, many respected spirit guides claim that coincidence has no place in the Divine Scheme of things, which is why they hitch their wagons firmly to the star of the Natural Laws, Laws which state that everything is ruled by the unbreakable dictate of *Cause and Effect*.

They claim that because of this Law, there can be no such thing as an accident or a coincidence.

Events happen because a sequence of *causes* puts into operation a corresponding sequence of *effects*.

For example, if a driver's brakes fail and he dies as a result of a terrible car-crash, this isn't an accident; everything happened according to the Laws. There were reasons *why* the brakes failed.

If a cable is severed, the laws of physics will ensure that the brakes won't work, and the scene is set for the tragedy to occur.

When discussing these esoteric claims, sceptics often bemoan the lack of scientific evidence to back them up, declaring that 'they can't be proved.'

But here's a thought: they can't be disproved, either.

Yet no one can dispute that down through the centuries countless people have touched the robe of death, but didn't pass over until a later date.

What do you think?

What is your philosophy?

One night, as a young lad sitting before a blazing coal fire in the 1960s, I remember my mother saying that in the Second World War she'd worked in a munitions factory, preparing thousands of bullet-cases for British Forces to use.

'Sometimes,' she recalled with a sigh, 'I'd stop work, lift up a bullet and think to myself: *I wonder whose name is written on this?*'

Discussion Topic:
Think back to an important time when you met someone who changed the course of your life: this could be a partner or someone who significantly influenced your pathway.

Now imagine what your life would be like today if you hadn't been there to meet them.

Do you think you would have met them anyway, at some later date? Do you think your pathways were destined to cross?

33

Reincarnation, Fate and Chance
Is Life Predestined?

This is an imperfect world peopled by imperfect beings who will make many mistakes during their lifetimes.

That's why souls come to the Earth, to expand their awareness through gaining experiences in all aspects of their spiritual, mental, emotional and physical lives.

Life is about growth; and none of us will have an easy time of it.

More than ever, a medium's role in today's world is to help man to realise that the Spirit World is the real world, that his Mind and Character are his only lasting possessions, and that materialism is a transient doctrine.

The world is filled with religions of all kinds but, ultimately, what a man calls himself is of little account; what really matters is what he does in this incarnation: how he thinks, acts, and treats other life-forms.

Without exception, all religions are man-made belief-systems, and there's an inherent danger in accepting the dictates in anyone's sacred writings as the absolute truth.

How does anyone know that his set of beliefs are stamped with Divine authority?

If we think this through, we'll realise that it will all come down to a question of belief and trust, to a question of faith.

People are told that their religious books have authority; people are impressed to believe that their book is a holy book, and that other faiths are misguided; but there is a great danger in intolerance, and particularly in religious intolerance.

Throughout history, religious intolerance has caused divisions, bloodshed, and untold carnage among many races.

We should think for ourselves, always, and believe whatever is reasonable, and reject what doesn't appeal to our intelligence.

Nearly all religions are based on a person's ability to have faith in what is taught to him; however, Spiritualism breaks this mould by trying to offer evidence of the soul's immortality.

But you must make your own investigations, and reach your own conclusions.

But if we *are* Everlasting and Indestructible, then we are energy, for energy cannot be destroyed. Therefore, as energy, we've had no beginning and we will have no end; though we may change our forms many times, for that's one of the properties of energy. If this is true you are likely to be an ancient being, and your present life cannot be your first existence and it might not be your last.

The doctrine of reincarnation teaches that we chose our present incarnations, with all their difficulties and trials, in order to quicken our soul growth.

As we watch horrific television pictures of wars and conflicts taking place around the globe, many of us must wonder, 'Why is this cruelty being perpetrated on those people?'

Why is it that you are able to read these words in the peace of your home, while elsewhere on the planet other souls are suffering and dying?

Why aren't *you* being targeted in an air-raid?

Are all these events planned?

Are we governed by Chance; or are we simply the playthings of Fate?

Discussion Topic:

If reincarnation is a fact: why did you choose to be born at this point in history?

What is your purpose for coming back into the Earthworld?

34

Can We See the Future?

When we look up into the dark sky on a winter's night we marvel at the panoply of stars, which look like glistening jewels sewn into the black velvet robe of God.

Billions of people have lain down on grassy clifftops and have felt humbled by the thought of the immense distances between themselves and the rest of this magnificent Universe.

But our naked eyes can look out only through our own vast galaxy, the Milky Way, which contains billions of stars.

We cannot see beyond this; neither can we see a living picture of our Universe as it is *at present*; we can see only a picture of the Universe *as it was*, in its past state, the Universe as it use to be, perhaps millions of years ago.

Starlight from distant suns takes a long time to reach the Earth and this distance is measured in light-years: one light-year being the time it takes a light-wave to reach us through space, travelling at approximately 186,000 miles per second.

The immensity of this speed is too staggering a thought to comprehend.

What appears in our night sky is nothing more

than a picture of a Time long gone, yet we can see it now.

The ever-faithful North Star barely moves in our hemisphere, but it's incredible to think that this Guide-Star might not exist now; for all we know, it could have exploded into a supernova decades ago.

Although we live in the present, we're able to look into the past – *right now*.

Consider now the Time Zones we've established around the planet's circumference.

When one nation finishes with the shadow of night, it immediately belongs to another; and some kingdoms sleep while others are just waking.

Time, as we measure it (chronologically, with clocks) is simply an Illusion.

Time certainly exists, and many claim it's the 4th dimension: objects have three dimensions (height, depth and width) but they exist in our conscious experience only because they're travelling through Time, which is the 4th dimension.

In the last millennium, the BBC in London transmitted its first radio programmes, which were received, enjoyed, and then their signals moved out into the Universe. But energy-waves are indestructible, so somewhere in outer space those first programmes can still be received by life-forms in some faraway galaxy.

If we ourselves could stand upon a distant star, because of the speed of light-waves we wouldn't see the Earth's sun as it is now, we'd see it as it used to be, millions of years ago, perhaps long after it had ceased to exist.

There are many theories put forward about the nature of Time, but these simple examples remind us that *what we see with our eyes may not necessarily be Absolute Reality, but only a pale reflection of it.*

Now take a giant leap forward, millions of years into the future, and imagine that an extremely sensitive alien is standing on that same distant star and is receiving psychic images and telepathic signals from *you*, and that he's actually seeing the projected energy-pictures of *your* life unfolding before his clairvoyant gaze.

This Alien Watcher could be aware of all your feelings, thoughts, troubles and trials, and could be experiencing your life-time 'as it happens': but you (in your physical self) would have been long-since dead and buried. This concept raises an intriguing philosophical problem.

Back on Earth today, it's well documented that some sensitive people have foreseen and predicted important world events, which subsequently occurred 'in the future'.

Does this mean that sensitives can experience 'the future' long before it actually materialises, only because somehow, somewhere, *the Future is already happening Now*?

It's as though our Future events are *already* occurring somewhere and are sending their shockwaves backwards in Time into our Present experience. These concepts raise far more questions than they answer: for if the Future is already happening *Now*, does this mean that our lives are predestined?

Discussion Topic:
If our lives are preordained: who preordained them?

If your life-span is fixed, along with all or some of the events along your pathway, what happens to your Freewill?

35

Shaping Tomorrow's People
Is Education the Key to Peace?

Children, and adults, love to have their own way, especially when others do their bidding.

The hidden child still speaks in us, but real life often drowns out its voice.

Huge sums of money are quite rightly spent teaching children the basic literacy and numeracy skills; these will be of immense value, but cramming children's heads with facts will never help them to live fulfilled lives in the real world.

Young children should be taught the art of learning to live together in peace. They should also be taught good citizenship.

Many argue that it's the parents' responsibility to teach their offspring respect for society and its members, but the educational system should help because badly behaved adults cannot teach their offspring what it means to be a kind and thoughtful, law-abiding citizen – so schools should do this.

I come from a poor background where some children were allowed to run wild instead of being brought up nurtured with love.

Where I came from, ignorant parents raised ignorant children, and the 'sins of the fathers' were visited onto future generations.

And this still happens today. I know of one family who have never sought to improve their minds; they're quite content to sell newspapers on street corners for the rest of their lives. There's nothing wrong with selling newspapers, but if that's the extent of their desire to further their education and life-experience, I think they might have a problem; and they definitely need good parenting skills.

In recent years, I've watched their children follow in their parents' footsteps, and now their grandchildren are parked in prams, ready to follow suit.

They're caught in an educational vacuum.

Schooling should help young people to become responsible adults; and teaching children about human nature and how all creatures should learn to live together in peace should occupy a far more important place in school-life than simply gaining essential qualifications.

Passing examinations doesn't help anyone to develop a spiritual outlook.

If all the Earth's past tyrants and dictators had discovered the pleasure of caring for others, the joy of expressing their love freely, and the happiness of people who live peaceably together, would there have been any wars?

Education starts at our mothers' knees: children need to experience positive and loving influences, today – right now.

If you have children or grandchildren, what kind of example are you setting for them to follow?

We all play an important part in peopling tomorrow's world with responsible, compassionate human beings.

Today's children are tomorrow's citizens, but what kind of citizens are we encouraging them to be?

Thankfully, I was privileged to share a loving relationship with my mother, who died of cancer when I was a sensitive young man of twenty. In fact, it was her tragic death and her startling spirit-return three months later which sparked off the burgeoning of my mediumship.

She appeared late one summer's evening and stood within a ball of golden light at the top our staircase, calling my name and beckoning me to join her; and I remember thinking, 'The woman I love is *alive*, not dead. And if *she's* survived, then *everyone* survives. I must tell the world.'

Powerful emotions, such as these, impress the mind deeply, and they can never be forgotten.

Thinking back now to the many lovely memories I have of my mother, I'm touched by the kindness she showed to everyone. I learned a lot from her.

She was a good citizen. She was always ready to offer the hand of friendship; she looked outwards at people who stood in need, and didn't spend too much time looking inwards, towards herself.

I wish there were more people like her.

She taught me a great deal about life, love, service, respect and tolerance.

If there's one phrase, one epithet I could place in memory of my mother's life, I think it's this:

She was kind.

What greater praise could be given about any life?

And what are our lives, themselves, but Living Prayers: conscious expressions of the God-Force that moves through all our words, thoughts and deeds. I share my spirit guide's viewpoint, when he says, 'The noble qualities of kindness and compassion are the hallmarks of an evolving soul.'

My mother dealt with everyone fairly and equally; and all the while, her younger son was watching. Her compassion seemed to light up the darkness and restore people's faith in the goodness of human nature.

It is by our example that we teach.

The truth of this statement remains constant, but it's often forgotten by people who preach one code of ethics, but practise another. It's only when we take stock of our lives that we realise what effect we've had on others; and this is what makes simple self-analysis such a constructive exercise.

We've all experienced a feeling of tension when a disagreeable person enters a room: some people look for the nearest exit. But does this happen whenever you make an appearance? What effect do you have on the lives of your fellow souls?

After I've taken my last breath here on Earth, if someone places a rose upon my grave for any small kindnesses I may have performed, I shall smile, knowing full well that the flower is also placed for my mother, for she showed me the Way.

May God bless her, and all others who've treated their children with kindness and respect; for a life filled with love is never forgotten.

Discussion Topic:
Is it possible to render service, or to do your daily tasks, without any thought of self-interest or of gaining recognition?

36

The Conduct of the Soul
Thoughts to Ponder

What really matters is how we live our lives.

When we pass over into the eternal world of the
spirit, we shall gravitate to the sphere of existence
we've earned for ourselves through the building of
our character and the evolution and expression of
our spiritual qualities.

All we shall take with us through the gateway
called 'death' is Ourselves – nothing more,
nothing less. There are no pockets in shrouds,
no status symbols or earthly aggrandisement on
the Other Side of Life. We shall take only our
minds and characters:
we shall take with us our state of soul-growth
and our morals,
which are reflections of our true selves.

Over in the Next World,
you won't be the person *you* think you are,
or the person *the world* thinks you are –
you'll be the person *you truly are*.

In your new life, you'll clearly see that
the only things that really mattered on Earth were:
how you lived your life;
how you thought;
and how you acted.

It's not what happens to you that matters most:
what counts is how you deal with it.

Our problems are our own;
they don't belong to the people in the next world
and therefore the solving of them is
our responsibility.

Man is Personally Responsible for
his actions and thoughts.
There can be no off-loading of your acts onto
another's shoulders;
that is morally and spiritually wrong.
The Universal Laws don't allow you to transfer
your spiritual burdens in such a way.
You alone must work out your own 'salvation'.

This Earthworld makes much of
pomp and ceremony,
and it treasures public acclaim as
a mark of importance.
But in the Greater World,
which we'll all one day inherit,
what you call yourself will be of
little account when measured against
what you really are,
and what you've actually done with your life.

These spiritual qualities are the only eternal
treasures that you can ever possess.

Discussion Topic:
*The spirit people teach us that Thoughts are Living
Things. What do you think they mean by this?*

37

What is 'Right', and What is 'Wrong'?
Morals and the Universal Laws

The terms 'good' and 'evil' are judgements that we
make about the behaviour of others. But do these
terms represent any absolute reality outside our
subjective thoughts?

Does the power of evil exist in its own right?

Does the power of good exist in its own right?

When we judge another person's deeds, surely we
are measuring them against our own moral codes.
Behaviour that is in line with our mental programming is acceptable to us, and actions that are out-
of-step with our moral standards might repulse us.

However, what is 'good' to one man might seem
positively 'evil' to another.

To the Christian Fundamentalist, mediumship is
'of the devil'; but to the medium, it is 'God-sent'.
(Interestingly enough, mediumship will function
no matter what people think of it because it's a
psychic science.)

If we'd been raised in eastern countries our
culture and laws would be different, and so would
our morals. In some nations, to steal an apple from
a trader results in the cutting off of your right
hand – severed at the wrist, and probably in
public.

To westerners this act seems barbaric.

Morals differ according to who we are, where we live, and how we are educated.

Many spirit guides refer to 'the still small voice of conscience' within us, which they call 'the ever-present Divine Monitor that guides mankind', and they maintain that this inner voice (or deep spiritual awareness) understands what is 'right' and what is 'wrong'.

In fact, the 'still small voice' isn't a voice at all, it's an inner soul-knowing of what is, and what isn't, in alignment with the Universal Laws that govern all areas of being.

While morals might change from soul to soul and from nation to nation, the Universal Laws that govern them do not: they will always remain constant.

Whenever we pronounce actions 'right or wrong' or 'good or evil' we're merely expressing our feelings about them; the actions themselves care nothing for our thoughts.

If an executioner severs a man's hand in an eastern marketplace, no matter what he feels about his deed, he acts within the scope of Natural Law, committing movements with a scimitar blade which will slice through bones and sinews because it's wielded with sufficient force.

The conscience of the executioner might tell him that his actions are 'right' because he's been raised in a culture that advocates the punishment he's meting out; therefore, his conscience won't be immediately disturbed by his deed; though it will be in his future life in the spirit world (for in that world, he will realise how much his actions affected his victim and made him suffer).

The Universal Laws are Impersonal: they favour no man, woman or beast; no nation, sect or creed above another. They operate with perfect and objective mathematical precision.

Human morals and motives, however, frequently change.

Morals belong to the realms of behavioural conditioning, mental programming, and to the culture in which you've been raised.

Motives are your personal thoughts and your subjective ideas.

Discussion Topic:
In a hospital ward there's only one crash-cart which is used to resuscitate heart-attack victims, and it stands exactly in the middle of a corridor.

Two patients suffer cardiac-arrests at precisely the same time. The patient at one end of the corridor is a ninety-year-old woman with no living relatives; the patient at the other end of it is a thirty-year-old politician who has a wife and three children.

You are in charge of the crash-cart, and you can take it to one patient only.

To whom do you take it; and why?

38

The Windows of the Soul

Whenever I meet a stranger, within a microsecond the main body of his character is conveyed to my mind via my auric-fields. Receiving this kind of psychic impression becomes second nature to people who've developed their sensitivity.

This kind of auric reading strengthens with use, and as a result of following a course of mental-awareness exercises.

Even atmospheres and other people's thought-forms, which can permeate rooms and buildings, can be registered by sensitives.

The exercise of these psychic skills is a necessary tool in the training-programmes of all budding mediums, for it's in the strengthening of these abilities that they develop their sensitivity, which in turn paves the way towards making mediumistic contact with discarnates.

Every medium must be psychic, but not every psychic is necessarily a medium: the ability to mediate is usually a natural progression which grows out of mastering your psychic ability.

Let's look at a famous example of psychic power in operation. In the Christian Bible, the Nazarene is said to meet a woman of Samaria at the Well, as written in The Book of John, Chapter 4:

Jesus saith unto her, Go, call thy husband, and come hither.

The woman answered and said, I have no husband. Jesus said unto her, Thou hast well said, I have no husband:

For thou hast had five husbands; and he whom thou now hast is not thy husband...

The woman then left her waterpot and went her way into the city, and saith to the men,

Come, see a man, which told me all the things that I ever did.

In this story it is obvious that the Nazarene psychically gleaned the above details from the woman's mind; no spirit-voice needed to reveal them.

Here's a good tip for those who are trying to master this art of psychic reading: without doubt, the eyes are the windows of the soul.

Your eyes reflect your thought-patterns because your physical body is a manifestation of the quality and character of your soul.

Everything that you are, and every thought and emotion that you experience, reacts upon, and will eventually shape, your physical body.

Your eyes can communicate hidden impressions to sensitives, who might see coded messages flash through them, almost imperceptibly.

Finely developed sensitives can 'move through' a subject's eyes and become aware of some of the secrets written in his soul.

Remember, too, that our minds are open to the spirit people: nothing is hidden, and all is known.

STEPHEN O'BRIEN

A medium friend of mine had a spirit guide who was an Arab horseman when he lived in the desert-lands, and one day he told her something that shook her to the core of her being.

He said, 'Your mind is as open to me as the Sahara Desert'.

This is a stunning and humbling thought.

Discussion Topic:
The camera never lies. Is this statement true?

Seeing is believing. Is this statement true?

When ten people witnessed a car-crash, each of them gave the police a different account of what happened. Why was this?

39

A Message of Encouragement
from the Spirit World

Delivered by Stephen O'Brien's spirit guide,
White Owl, Christmas 1991

From our world of light we send greetings to your
plane of thought.

Often your lives are full of struggle and hardship,
but we are standing beside you all of the way.

Each faltering step you take is known by
someone in these Greater Worlds beyond Earth.

However, it is not our function to take away your
full responsibility for choices, or to remove your
right to govern your soul's destiny through its
many trials and lifetimes.

We are here simply to advise, to guide, and
sometimes to point out the pathways that are
available to you as you progress down through the
ages.

We are assigned to our friends, encased in flesh,
by the power of love. We have lived a long time,
and we know how to draw near to bless and guide
you whenever we can.

We feel able to help you because our longevity
affords us much wider viewpoints; one cannot live
many centuries and not change one's perspectives
on life, for with time the mind sharpens and
expands its awareness, and eventually one grows

in wisdom.

From our world we can often see, more clearly than you, what lies ahead of you in your journeys of the soul. Based upon our experience we can therefore state that Peace and Love are found within the soul which is trying to progress towards the mastery of its Self.

Eventually, the grosser animal-like qualities become more refined as the soul moves forward through the scale of evolution, until it steps upon the ladder of Thought known as Man.

But only when you come into our side of life will you really appreciate where you have come from, why you were incarnated on Earth, and what lies ahead of you.

At this time when many in your world remember the man whom some call 'The Prince of Peace', our message to you is this: write across the pages of your mind, soul, and personality, these words: love, peace, kindness of thought, and harmlessness.

These are good starting-points from which a more enlightened and peaceful existence with yourself and with other lives may be achieved.

We cannot walk the path for you – you alone must undertake your own soul-growth and progression; this is your responsibility.

But we can be beside you, helping and perhaps inspiring you towards the Light; advising you that there is no lasting joy in the darkness of ignorance, hatred, racialism, anger or apathy.

Go forward into your future with confidence, fully knowing that we will never fail you.

Others may let you down, forsake you and forget you, but we will never leave you comfortless.

We are as constant as the Northern Star in our efforts to uplift you, to share our knowledge with you, and to guide all those who have dedicated their lives in service to their neighbours.

Those who serve are often closest to our hearts and thoughts, for they are walking the hardest pathway.

Rendering service is not easy; and the more enlightened a soul is, the greater is the service it is called upon to perform. It has to be that way: tough tasks are not for the weak but for the strong, for the experienced, the dedicated, the faithful and the true.

These are the Laws of Life.

Knowledge always precedes the coming of greater and wider responsibilities.

Knowledge increases awareness; awareness heightens sensitivity, and this informs the mind that Love is the Greatest Power. So use it, share it, give it freely to all those in need of it; for only in the giving does the soul truly receive its reward.

At the end of one year and the beginning of the next, sometimes sad reflections fall upon your minds. Gently recognise these and then banish them, replacing them with cheerful optimism and light: the light of our love for you all.

We reaffirm our promise: *we will never fail you. And whenever you step forward to serve, a thousand souls here in my world will step behind you, to aid you.*

Never doubt our presence - we are just a thought away.

Put your trust in the unseen guiding light of God, the Great Spirit. He has not forsaken you; and neither we will we, His ministers.

Magnificent Spirit of Life, for all your blessings,
both hidden and seen,
we render our grateful thanks.

And may Great Peace be with you...

Discussion Topic:
*Where was God when Mount Vesuvius erupted and
all but wiped out the population of ancient Pompeii?*

40

Spiritual Darkness and Light
Stephen O'Brien's spirit guide speaks on the Law

Each soul is personally responsible for the growth-rate and expansion of its spiritual nature as it evolves through the experiences gained in many incarnations.

During the journey, everything of which the individual can be aware exists only within that soul's fields of consciousness, and no experience can ever originate from some mysterious place regarded by that individual as 'outside' himself.

All is within.

We who have lived a very long time have learned the truth of many spiritual laws, and one of these states that knowledge and inspiration can come only to those who have earned the right to receive them. The complex outworking of the Great Spirit's Divine Plan, which is the blueprint for the overall spiritual progression of mankind, ensures that no life is overlooked or neglected: all receive exactly what they have earned for themselves.

Not one jot more (or less) Justice, Retribution or Reward can be reaped than has been sown by each soul.

When people look deeply into the current difficulties surrounding them, they must realise that these challenges were created by no other influence than themselves: you personally attract each soul-test into the orbit of your consciousness.

There is a time and place for everything, and nothing happens by accident, for everything functions within the scope of the Natural Laws that encompass every facet of being.

If a soul should find itself in Darkness, it is because it has not yet learned to seek and know the Light.

But no soul will be left comfortless in its quest for evolution, for the Great Spirit will see to it that signs and guidance along the route will always be in evidence.

As you travel the road of your destiny, unfolding your spiritual awareness and blending more fully with your spiritual consciousness, all manner of gurus will serve as guideposts to you: they will act as catalysts that will open within your mind new tracks of thought.

Each voice you hear, vocally or silently, no matter how humble its origin, has something to teach you: it will either inspire you directly with its knowledge of spiritual verities, or impart its wisdom in a meaningful glance, a guiding thought, or in the written form.

However, all those who earnestly seek to realise the Presence of the Great Spirit will learn that the answers to all of their questions are to be found only within their own fields of consciousness.

When the soul reaches certain landmarks in the evolution of its spiritual nature, it will have earned for itself the right to experience several instantaneous realisations.

If a man locks himself away in a mental 'dungeon' created by his own negative thoughts and blinkered vision, and then one day his cell doors are suddenly opened and someone enters with a lighted candle, the prisoner's darkness cannot exist where there is light, and the darkness is instantly dispersed.

When the light comes, those who have thus imprisoned themselves will have two choices: either they can gratefully accept the light of truth and never again dwell in the darkness of ignorance, or they can snuff out the flame, thereby losing a golden opportunity to discover their inner selves for what they truly are.

We, in the spirit, consider it a privilege to hand to mankind such a lighted flame.

If you will accept this illumination from us, and then, in your turn, pass it on to other souls who are ready to receive it, you will help us to effect the spiritual advancement of mankind.

Discussion Topic:
Think of something that is very dear to you: a person, an idea, a belief, or a sentimental possession.

As part of your journey of self-discovery, you visit the world's wisest guru and ask him, 'What must I do in order to progress spiritually?'

He answers, 'You must free yourself of desire. You must give up the one thing that is dearest to you, and must never again have any contact with this treasured possession as long as you live upon the Earth.'

Could you do it?

And if not: why not?

Understanding the God-Power Within You

41

Some Thoughts on The Nature of God

Seeking evidence to prove the existence of God has taxed some of the greatest minds for millennia, and today's philosophers are still seeking it: some believe in an Almighty Power, and others don't.

But what do you believe?

*

The Last Total Eclipse of the Sun of the 2nd Millennium,
on 11th August 1999, as seen from the UK

The momentous occasion of the last total eclipse of the sun before the start of the third millennium was witnessed by an estimated three hundred million people across the globe. As one of these, I stood on a beach in Swansea, South Wales, with special solar-viewers held to my eyes, and for me the whole event was a spiritual experience.

Dawn broke miserably in Great Britain on that Wednesday, with cloud cover so thick that many of us despaired we'd see anything at all; but Nature took a turn in our favour, as you'll see...

Further south, in Cornwall, millions of people, including hordes of scientists and astronomers, were dismayed by the virtually impenetrable cloudbanks high above them; the leaden-grey skies rained down, and many feared they would glimpse nothing of the eclipse.

We later discovered that South Wales turned out to be one of the better places in Great Britain from which to see this remarkable event, and we were told that in our region 97% of the sun would vanish behind the moon.

From about 9.30 a.m. hundreds of people started gathering all along the Welsh beach: people from all walks of life arrived in cars, on motorbikes, and on foot to see the promised spectacle. It seemed that everyone wanted to be there.

In fact, millions of people around the world wanted to watch as the Great Forces of Nature moved the moon across the face of the sun.

On Swansea Bay, mothers wheeled their toddlers in pushchairs up the grassy banks and then down onto the sands, and dads and couples linked up with single people of all ages – we all seemed drawn towards the shoreline on that morning.

One man, who was over ninety years old, and who'd witnessed the last British Total Eclipse on 29th June 1927, was helped out of a car by his daughters and grandchildren. Aided by loved ones and two stout walking-sticks, and with his back bent by age and infirmity, he ambled slowly forward to get a prime position on the beach.

Back in 1927, special eclipse-viewers weren't widely available, so most people had looked at the sun through pieces of glass clouded with candle-smoke. But today, this old man had come well prepared and he held on tightly to his special glasses.

Geographically, we'd be just outside what's known as 'The Tract of Totality', so we weren't expecting to experience the total darkness that was promised to engulf the tip of Cornwall; nevertheless, we knew from the mathematically precise calculations of astronomers that we'd fall just outside the moon's shadow (its umbra), and that we'd experience 97% of 'Totality' (because we were in the moon's penumbra, which is its semi-shadow area).

But that didn't dampen our spirits or our enthusiasm; we'd be just 3% away from the full eclipse and we couldn't believe our luck.

While waiting for first contact (that remarkable moment when the moon first touches the edge of the sun's disc) I was reminded of Spielberg's film, *Close Encounters of the Third Kind*, in which many psychic people felt compelled to be present at a special meeting-place.

The sky on the horizon began to turn a clear blue and its brightness was approaching us; but the moment of first contact was denied us, it seemed, because the high cloud-cover held fast. However, it did break many times and we saw an amazing sight that wouldn't be repeated again in Great Britain until the year 2,090.

Like many others who witnessed this strange but natural event, I can't describe my feelings of amazement, humility, respect, and wonder at the great creative processes at work before my eyes.

Thinking back to that morning now, the crowds were remarkably patient, the atmosphere was very still, and there was a strong current of expectation rippling through the air.

Throughout the next hour or so, we had dozens of opportunities to view the eclipse as it progressed to 97% cover – and we took them all gladly.

I think my psychic sensitivity came into play when I studied the sun because I could clearly see the outline of its bright corona, which we aren't supposed to see until Totality reveals it.

People of all ages watched, fascinated, as the sun's disc was gradually 'eaten away' by the slow-moving bulk of the moon; and every few minutes, they gasped in wonderment.

At approximately 11.14 a.m. the huge shadow of the moon sped over our part of the Earth and rushed towards us from the west, bringing with it a darkening of the light. It wasn't like twilight, which has a richness of golds and blues in it, this darkness was an eerie negation of light.

As our eyes turned towards the sun, the land beneath our feet fell under the shadow of the moon's penumbra (which was hundreds of miles in diameter) and gradually bright daylight turned into evening – in the middle of the morning.

The iron-grey clouds above us looked as if a great thunderstorm were gathering behind them, and the moon's shadow cast a coppery-orange glow over everything, which fascinated us.

Suddenly the beach became quiet.

The temperature dropped, and then the breeze strengthened.

I felt cold.

And then the light faded quickly to its darkest.

It was so eerie...

Seagulls cried out over the distant water, but we

were stunned into silence – except for some people who couldn't help whispering to their companions. 'My God...' 'This is absolutely incredible...' 'Amazing...' 'I've never seen anything like this before...'

Everyone was affected by the event; and even those who had no eye-protection were fortunate enough to witness the amazing phenomenon because whenever a thin layer of cloud veiled the sun, the eclipse was clearly visible to the naked eye.

A jittery young lad of about eight had been squinting at the sun without any protection, an act which could have caused him blindness, so I handed him my viewers and his eyes sparkled with joy. He tilted his head towards the sky... and was so affected by what he saw that he stood absolutely still, and looked and stared, and gazed at the copper-coloured heavens.

'This is a day for you to remember,' I said to him, 'something to tell your children and your grand-children about when you're old and grey: a once-in-lifetime event.'

'Oh, yes,' he said, his voice full of wonder. 'I'll never forget this.'

In fact, I lent my solar-viewers to a number of people to experience the phenomenon and they, too, were dumbstruck by the event.

I was enthralled by the eclipse; it was only later that I wept when I saw the whole event broadcast on television and heard hundreds of thousands of people in dozens of countries across the world cheering, clapping, whistling and crying with joy as the shadow of absolute Totality passed over their heads, when the sun's bright corona or halo of light was briefly revealed during Totality...

Then, two minutes and twenty-three seconds later, the sky brightened again, and quickly returned to normal.

It was over much too soon... and as I looked across the Bay I saw the skies darkening over the eastern coastline as the massive penumbra rushed past the headland at 1,500 miles per hour...

In my quiet moments, when I recall the eclipse, a few thoughts occur to me:

Who among us had the power to prevent that remarkable event from happening? Could anyone have stopped it?

The answer is *no*: not one of us.

On that late summer's morning, like millions of others I was deeply impressed by the Majesty of Nature and by the Magnificence of The Immutable Natural Laws in operation before my eyes.

We, who believe ourselves to be so sophisticated and intelligent, can only stand and stare at such incredible natural phenomena – and marvel at the awesome power displayed.

Discussion Topic:

We each have a Guardian Angel watching over us.

Is this statement true?

What about rapists, criminals and murderers? Are they guarded by Angels?

And if they are: what kind of Angels are protecting them?

And what about the victims of crime and tyranny? Are they also watched over by Guardian Souls?

And if they are: where were these Guardian Souls when these victims were suffering or in pain?

42

God and The Creative Will

Do you believe in God?
Yes, unequivocally – I see God as a sentient all-encompassing power.

Do you think God has a personality?
Yes.

God created everything: there's only One Power in the Universe and nothing can exist outside this Vast Consciousness, this Great Oversoul.

Because this Great Spirit is present in every personality It has ever created, Its 'Personality' can be discovered Everywhere and in every thing.

God is a Great Power, and not a person; and the Energy of God is in our Universe, which is a living entity in a state of constant change; it's forever evolving, just as we are, and just as I believe The Great Spirit is.

To discover the personality of God we should examine the Pageant of Life and Consciousness teeming all around us and within us, for it's there that His Composite Nature may be found.

So is God 'Our Father', or 'Our Mother', or both?
Both: God is All Things.

The Great Spirit is an androgynous Power that contains both masculine and feminine aspects within It, and this is reflected in the world of sexuality, which is why we, who have the Spirit of God within us, are androgynous in essence.

Each soul possesses 'male' and 'female' psychic energies, no matter what its sexual characteristics may be, and some people express the masculine (or more forceful) energies, while others manifest the feminine (or more gentle) spiritual forces.

Some spirit guides claim that the Great Spirit is, in fact, the Natural Laws. What are your thoughts on this?
It's illogical to confine the omnipresent Spirit of God merely to a set of Natural Laws, for Infinite Intelligence cannot be subject to finite boundaries.

Spirit guides point to the precision and majesty of the Natural Laws because they consider them to be powerful expressions of God's Power and his Creative Will. The Laws, they say, are intelligent manifestations of the Great Spirit's presence in all things.

When spirit guides teach that God is an all-powerful, all-knowing, ever-present Spirit which motivates every atom within each animate and inanimate form, I believe they're trying to cultivate within man a reverence and respect for Life itself.

We cannot be anywhere that God is not.

We are parts of God. We're not cut asunder from Him: this is an impossibility, for God's Spirit is within us.

We are Children of the Living God.

God Is Everything That Is. God is All.

To perceive this, one requires a depth of soul-sensitivity and spiritual awareness.

Who created me?
You exist only because The Great Spirit dreamed you into existence. You've been created to live out a life within the framework of a Divine Plan, which The Supreme Power has formulated and is now outworking through all the life-forms It has brought into being.

You've also been given the power of Freewill, but the exercise of this power is limited by sets of complex Natural Laws, which were also created by The Great Spirit.

For example: you can't flap your arms and expect to fly to the moon; you can't drink the sea dry in one gulp; you can't perform complicated mental gymnastics if your thinking is slovenly and your mind is lazy.

Man's Freewill is forever limited by spiritual, physical, mental, and emotional laws.

But we aren't puppets: we're co-creators with God because The Power is evolving *through* us, Its creations.

And The Great Spirit has darker energies within Its nature, too – just as we have. Indeed, we're but pale reflections of our Creator's omnipresent mind.

Why do so many people seek a soulmate, someone with whom they might feel a spiritual affinity?
To balance the deeper spiritual and psychic energies within their personalities, people try to 'complete' the picture of their sexuality. Males seek females, and vice versa. However, some gentle

men might seek out more masculine males as companions; and some masculine females might seek more feminine women, in an effort balance their psychic energies.

However, if people searched deeply within themselves they'd find all the power they need to balance their soul-energies, which would negate the search for outside stimuli.

Do you think man's Freewill can overpower and thereby negate the Will of God?
No. God's Will continuously presses through the minds of all the life-forms It has created. There's only one authority: the omnipotent, omniscient, omnipresent God; the all-powerful, all-knowing, present-in-all-places-at-the-same-time Creative Spirit of Consciousness-Being, and none can overpower His Almighty Will.

'Nature is red in tooth and claw' because some under-developed parts of God's Spirit are still struggling to evolve their characters through living in this world of matter; they're slowly progressing towards the state of Perfect Love.

How can I get closer to God?
You're already linked to the Creative Mind, for ever.

You can never be separated from your Creator – the link remains eternally unbroken.

We are Sons and Daughters of the Living Mind, and therefore we're all Brothers and Sisters.

Is God Love?
Countless billions of people have thought of God as

a Power of Love, but many ancient philosophers believed that the One Soul expresses Itself through the three powers of *Creation, Preservation and Destruction* (or *Transformation*).

Millions of people cannot accept God only as a Power of Love, for they recognise Its Destructive quality in the Natural World, in which objects are broken down into their elements, sometimes by cataclysmic forces, only to be later gathered together again to form new creations.

When a supernova explodes, its gases, dustclouds and star debris are atomised and propelled into space by incredibly powerful forces.

These particles later mingle with other material and suddenly collapse inwards under the weight of great mass towards a central point, and thus a new star is born.

The Creator's Universe is a living entity in a state of constant flux, forever progressing and slowly evolving through the multifarious experiences occurring within it.

The Spirit of God is forever recycling Itself.

God is also believed by many to be the Origin of Love, Peace, Joy, Beauty, Stillness, and Light.

How can I achieve a lasting sense of spiritual happiness?

Be cheerful, release your anxieties about your future and allow yourself to be swept along by the mighty Tide of God's Power and spontaneous Inspiration.

Don't battle against the Current.

The Power has set down a pattern for your life and has given you the energy and intelligence to follow it.

You are exactly where you're supposed to be; you're the person you were meant to be – and the conditions you're now experiencing were designed to accelerate your spiritual progression.

Just 'Go with the flow', and do your best to make as much progress as possible.

Life flows unceasingly like the current of a great river: sometimes the waters move in fast frantic torrents; at other times they glide slowly and peacefully, but they can still surprise us by twisting around unexpected bends.

The happiest souls are those who've learned to swim with the current.

Do accidents, tragedies, murders and killings occur with God's permission?
Nothing can ever be separated from the all-encompassing Infinite Spirit of God.

There are no such things as accidents in this vast panorama of Being, which is governed by Supreme Intelligence.

All pain and suffering, all seeming injustice, and the many other ills associated with life in the world of matter, including the violent or the early ending of a physical life, are tragedies only when viewed from a material standpoint.

The one who makes the crossing doesn't think it's a tragedy to have died because he finds himself still alive in a world of light.

Spiritually enlightened souls try to see their trials and challenges as opportunities for growth and spiritual progression.

Why do you teach that the Earthplane is 'the shadow-world'?

There's only One Reality and that is the Great Oversoul, all else is a reflection cast by the beams of light from this Shining Flame.

Man regards Earthlife as of prime importance and he relegates the two other aspects of his being (his mind and his spirit) into second and third position – and this action sows within him the seeds of illusion and self-deception, which can quickly produce misery and sorrow.

Earthlife is simply a shadow-dance cast by the Light of God through a slow-vibrating veil of misty matter. Just like a film on a cinema screen, man's Earth-existence is a set of transient kaleidoscopic images playing themselves out in a preconceived Cosmic Dream: but this dream appears to him as objective reality.

Discussion Topic:

Where do you go when you're asleep?

What happens to you in deep sleep, when you're completely unaware of what transpires around your body in the bedroom, and to all intents and purposes you are unconscious?

What happens to you during an operation when your body is anaesthetised?

Where do 'you' go?

43

The Great Silence

Man rushes through his existence filling every moment with activities that prevent him from finding the stillness within The Great Silence, which is a deep and tranquil state known as 'the peace that passes all understanding'.

Why are so many people afraid of silence and of being alone?

Man has conditioned himself; he fills his time with activity to distract his attention from the real problems in his life, and this practice is known as 'displacement activity'.

We're all familiar with the highly-strung woman who seeks the love and respect of her peers and therefore can't say 'No' to their demands.

This kind of person suffers from an anxiety complex, which, in simple terms, is an inner power-struggle between Duty and Desire.

The duties that she feels she must perform can often be secretly powered by her desires to gain love and acceptance, as compensation for a deep-seated sense of unworthiness, a state which may have been programmed into her child-mind by ignorant guardians.

Such a woman can't sit still without fiddling with

her teacup, or smoking a cigarette 'to relieve stress', even though she fears the fatal risks of tobacco addiction.

Displacement activities are generated by the mind, that master illusionist, which fills the screen of consciousness with anything to prevent us from looking at some of the darker life-challenges that are often painful to face.

To break these powerful illusions we can identify each displacement activity and then cease to perform it; we will then have to accept ourselves as we truly are. But this is easier said than done. However, without this confrontation no significant peace of mind can be found.

Only by disempowering our illusions and then by deepening our sense of calmness will The Great Silence reveal itself to us.

This blessing of peace cannot be gained only by affirming self-hypnotic suggestions such as, 'I must be at peace with myself', 'I will now become the silence', or 'My thoughts will now be still'. The Profound Stillness I'm speaking of is a Living Sense of Being that can be found only when we remove every shadow of illusion that veils the Depth of Tranquillity from our sight.

Those who have successfully touched the Great Silence bear its hallmarks: they're balanced, gentle beings who are at peace with themselves, and who, because of this, radiate kindness and a healing presence into the atmosphere around them.

These advanced souls remain undisturbed by fits of frenzied anger; and because they've touched the Silence they don't suffer from anxiety, for they've realised a state of Bliss within themselves.

Here, then, is the goal of spiritual development: to attain a full realisation of the only imperishable relationship that you will ever experience: your spiritual, eternal security is to be found in the Love of the Great Spirit, and this Love is within you.

Through contemplation and meditation we can experience great peace and silence, and learn to love it so much that we desire its constant healing presence. And each one of us will then realise the following truth:

> The most important relationship you will ever have, is the one that you have with yourself.

In The Great Silence, we find not only God but also the Kingdom of Heaven within us.

> 'Be still, and know that I AM God'.

Discussion Topic:
Do you think there are any profound spiritual reasons which might explain why newborn babies cry?

44

We Belong to the Stars

From ancient stardust we are made:
    galaxy-children birthed afar;
    mentalities castawayed,
    invisible to the naked eye,
    uncountable, unweighed,
yet beating like the heart of an avatar
as every life-note's played.

We belong to the stars, you and I,
fashioned by Living Breath long-since:
    from a timeless nothing
    sprang liquid thought
    which breathed and burned
    genetic fingerprints.

An Infinite Spirit exploded Its Mind:
dispersing suns and sentient clouds;
    warming blood and sprinkling souls
    as stardust gifts
    through hands of stone
    and hearts of flint.

From only One came the All that Is:
an Oversoul breathed out Its Thought;
    and back to Alpha we must return —
    heartaches,

journeys,
  starlight dreams –
    from beginning to end
      the soul will yearn.

45

Thought and Belief
Ideas for discussion

There are many great world religions
but, in truth, there is only one true religion:
Service and Love

The word 'Religion' is derived from the Latin
religere, meaning, 'to bind again',
which refers to the ancient religious practice of
joining together souls living in two
separate states of life –
one in the physical world and the other
in the world of the spirit.

Your religion should provide you with a basic moral
blueprint for the way in which to live your life.

Love One Another – and Serve One Another

When you reach the next world,
what you profess to believe will be of little account
when it's measured against
what you've actually done in your life.

What truly matters to the human spirit
is the way in which you have thought and behaved
towards yourself and others.

Everything you think, say and do
is indelibly registered upon the fabric of your soul –
and it makes you the person you truly are.

There is no cheating the Perfect Eternal Natural Laws,
which are created by God,
The Great Spirit of All Life.

We earn our places in Eternity by *what we are*
and by *what we've done* in our Earthlives.

Divine Justice rules this universe.

All roads lead to God;
but the way we live our lives is more important than
the name of the road we're travelling on,
for we shall change direction many times in
our search for truth.

If your religion makes you a better person,
then it's right for you.
If it teaches you to love,
then it's a good set of instructions.

If you believe in anything one hundred per cent
this is unhealthy, because your mind is then
closed to any new possibilities.

The people on the Other Side of life
aren't concerned with labels,
religions or lip-service codes of conduct;
they're concerned with souls, not labels.

Before you help someone, don't ask them what religious faith they hold, because these aren't the most important facets of our lives.

Discussion Topic:
It is possible to be a morally good person without practising any religion.
  Is this statement true?

46

The Great Spirit

And in bewildering confusion, Man looked up and cried out from the depths of his Being, 'God, who art Thou?'
And as silent as a whisper upon the wind there came a mind-voice, saying:

I Am all that Is.
  I Am in all things,
Through all things,
  Behind all things:
The Fire of Life
  Within a babe;
I shine behind your lover's eyes,
  A Power, crystallised.

I Am the Positive
And the Negative,
  Good and Bad;
  Love and Hate.
I Am black and white
  And a myriad shades of grey.
I Am in the rolling thunder
and the fire-fly's light;
  I Am the morning
  And the night;
The Darkness and the Light.

See me in soft gentility,
  And also in every cruel act:
For I Am Everywhere,
  In Everything;
  Within all life-forms
    no matter what they lack.

Neither male nor female I,
  But Spirit, Soul, Consciousness,
  A pulsing Breath of Life and Mind:
    The Beginning, which never was;
    The fleeting Now;
    And the very End –
      which man will never find.

Discover Me in a flowering bud
  Or glimpse Me in a looking-glass;
I Am the Unlovable;
  The Untouchable; The Intolerable –
In Everything which comes to pass.

The 'Is' Am I:
  A set of Laws,
  Laid down fast, Immutable,
  Unchangeable keys to all doors.
I Am discompassionately Sublime,
  Mathematically Perfect;
  I Am the Beater of Time.

And those attuned to Me,
  Harmoniously,
  Find peacefulness and ease;
But to those ignoring Me
    comes disharmony
    and dis-ease.

For I Am all Causes and their precise Effects:
  I Am inside the All
And outside the Everything you know;
  I fill the Nothing,
And yet I Am the Nothingness also.

And I need no worship or genuflection
Nor petty appeasement;
  For I Am not an 'I' —
  I simply Am all things:
And you are my reflection.

And unto you is granted
A measure of My Power,
  For use, according to your Willing;

For You and I are One —
And We are Mind,
Evolving.

*

(Read my book *Angels By My Side*, for a fuller
discussion and examination of 'The One Living God'.)

PART FOUR

The Power of your Mind and Thought

Important Notes from the Author

In such a limited space, it would be impossible to discuss the vast subject of your mind and its close relationship to the processes of Thought, so in this section I'll simply highlight, and sometimes challenge, what I hope will be some interesting and intriguing philosophical questions.

47

The Mind and Thought

The Power of Thought controls our lives, but what is Thought? And what is its relationship to the Mind?

And what about our perceptions? Can we trust them; and will they always serve us well?

Once a Thought occurs in your mind, it immediately becomes a past experience; the moment after its birth your Thought ceases to be new and it passes into the realm of Memory.

Your Memory can therefore be considered as a personal storehouse of your records of the past: 'old' thoughts and images are being kept alive within you by that mysterious entity known as the Mind.

Your Mind is a capacity, a vehicle through which your thoughts may manifest, and within which they seemingly 'live'. When a new experience befalls you it's registered by Thought and is then compared with previous memories so that you may understand it; after which all new experiences quickly become more old Thoughts which are added to your memory-banks.

If you wish to unfold your spiritual nature you must free yourself from the crippling strangle-hold of much of your past mental, emotional, and spiritual conditioning. Your mind has created each of the mental images you've stored within you, and you are the one who empowers them to sometimes distort your perception of reality.

To know yourself for what you really are is the vital first step on the road towards changing your character; and this can be accomplished only through a simple process of self-enquiry:

Man know thyself.

The deeper man delves into his consciousness, the more he realises how much more spiritual development awaits his attention. Gazing outwards into the physical world (the phenomenal world) to find the answers to some of life's great mysteries is often a frustrating quest: to discover the spiritual answers, we must turn within.

A clear inward vision reveals to us that we can lay the blame for our ills at the feet of no one else but ourselves.

Some philosophers argue that *everything* exists within us, and that we have created our own objective world which we can see, sense and feel.

Spirit guides sometimes advocate that in order to unfold our spiritual natures we must 'die' to all the crippling psychological conditioning of our past; we must 'die' to many of the irrational fears born of ignorant yesterdays.

Once we're free of much of our crippling and negative past programming our inward vision becomes clearer, and we can then prepare the way for further personal assessment.

Living in the past holds your soul in bondage, whereas existing in the ever-present Now can set your spirit free.

Until man learns to exist in the reality of the present moment – until he learns to live in the continuous time-stream of the Eternal Now – he may remain nothing more than a bundle of old Thoughts and Memories, which, if unchecked, might continue to breed misery and sorrow within his Mind.

Discussion Topic:

What are your thoughts on euthanasia, or 'mercy-killing'?

Is it right to terminate a life, in any circumstances?

What are your thoughts on abortion? Do we have the right, in any circumstances, to terminate the life of an unborn child?

Although the final decision usually rests with the mother, what would you do if you were that person, and you'd been raped by a violent criminal? Would you carry the criminal's child and give birth to it?

If you would: why would you do this?

And if you wouldn't: why wouldn't you do this?

48

The Perceiver and the Perceived

Let's take a look at this philosophical statement: *nothing exists outside yourself*.

You are a Perceiver, and your mind meets each new experience by instantly comparing it with similar images and feelings that you've already experienced and stored in your memory.

Your mind is a bundle of 'old' memories and Thoughts, and is filled with powerful images of past psychological responses; but every new experience is also made up of a group of similar images and impressions. Therefore, we're now in a position to say that what is Perceived – a bundle of images registered by Thought – is exactly the same in essence as the Perceiver's mind, which is also made up of a similar bundle of Thoughts.

It's not unreasonable to state now that in essence, *The Perceiver is also The Perceived*.

Think about this for a few moments before reading on. Read the above paragraphs again until you can clearly see the connection between the Perceiver and what it is that he Perceives:

Everything is Thought. If you remove the Thinker; there can be no Thought. And if you remove the Thought, you remove the Thinker's knowledge of his existence.

If you remove 'the Perceiver' (*you*), as you do when you're in a state of deep and dreamless sleep, or when you're unconscious, then you also remove what is physically Perceived (*your experiences*).

But when the Perceiver regains consciousness, what he Perceives simultaneously springs back into existence with him.

This theory raises deep philosophical questions, not the least of which is the following:

If the Perceiver is also the Perceived, does this mean that nothing actually exists outside your mind?

For instance, when you leave your house and walk around the corner to visit a friend: is your house still there where you left it? Does your house exist when you're not there to see it? Or does it spring into existence only when you need to see it, when you require it to be there for you?

Is your house part of a real physical world which will exist whether or not you're there to see it and experience it?

Is there an absolute reality called the objective world all around us, or do our minds create it with our thoughts?

Is this book a real object that is 'outside' yourself, or does it exist only within your mind because you feel the need to reassure yourself by reading it?

Your mind-images are certainly 'within' you – and your perceptions are also 'within' you; but does this mean that everything you perceive has its existence only *within* your Self? (After all, you cannot know with any certainty what another soul might be experiencing).

These are thought-provoking questions, to which you can try to find the answers.

But before we conclude this train of thought let's now take another philosophical leap and state that if all of the above is true, then your anger is you; your love is you; your hatred, cruelty and jealousy are you; your joys, sorrows and sufferings are you; the process of your spiritual development is also you, and therefore you alone are responsible for unfolding it.

And if all these things, and more, make up what is known as 'you' – then what exactly are you?

Discussion Topic:

Do you think modern society should live by the Ten Commandments, which were said to have been given to Moses by God, and upon which, arguably, some of the western world's system of Law is based?

Give your reasons for accepting or rejecting each of the following modernised 'rules':

1 *You shall have no other gods before me.*
2 *You shall not make for yourself any graven image.*
3 *You shall not take the name of the Lord your God in vain.*
4 *Remember the Sabbath day and keep it holy.*
5 *Honour your father and your mother.*
6 *You shall not kill.*
7 *You shall not commit adultery.*
8 *You shall not steal.*
9 *You shall not bear false witness against your neighbour.*
10 *You shall not crave to possess any thing that is your neighbour's.*

49

The 'I-Thought', or 'Body-Consciousness'

Man is keenly aware of his body, and believes he's a physical frame with many intangible Thoughts occurring within his head.

This kind of exclusive attention given to the flesh has been termed 'body-consciousness'.

I call this body-consciousness the 'I-thought', and it's the cause of much of man's pain and sorrow because with a multitude of clever mental illusions it veils from his awareness an understanding of his complete Self.

I-thoughts are self-centred energies that are deeply rooted in concern for the physical body's life and wellbeing, and they express themselves through feelings which make us say things like: *I'm sad; I'm lonely; I want pleasure; I must avoid pain; I'm sick; I'm unhappy; Why me? I need companionship*, etc.

It is the physical body that gives rise to these emotions, and this can be realised when we enquire of ourselves: *Who is it that is sad and lonely? What is it that desires pleasure? And what is it that wants to avoid pain? Who is it that is unhappy and lonely?*

But you are not just a physical body: the vast

amount of survival evidence supplied through mediumship demonstrates this. Mediumship proves that man's emotions, mind and spirit are not encased within a finite skull: he controls his body from a point somewhere beyond his brain.

The seat of consciousness is not the brain.

The brain is merely a thought-receiving and transmitting station that we use while we are associated with physical flesh. The pianist isn't the piano, and the composer isn't the song; and in the same way: your mind isn't your body.

However, the I-thought is a clever illusionist: it veils your true nature from you and tricks you into believing that your consciousness is pigeon-holed into four areas known as the superconscious, the conscious, the subconscious mind, and the body; whereas, in fact, you aren't fragmented at all – you're one complete entity.

The mighty I-thought fixes man's attention firmly in the physical world, and it enslaves the lives of billions of people, particularly in the demanding area of personal relationships where its power frequently generates chaos.

Those who seek spiritual development must recognise that a love of the objective world of matter, with all its false promises of lasting happiness, should be equally balanced by a love of the inner realm of the soul, in which is found the eternal Kingdom of Heaven.

It is in the everlasting realms of the spirit that Spiritual Love resides.

Only within yourself can you find Heaven, for it's a state of being and not a location somewhere 'out there'; it's an inner sense of freedom from all fear and illusion.

Through persistent and simple self-enquiry the soul may attain a degree of awareness that allows it to focus on The Central Source of Peace, on the place in which eternal tranquillity, equilibrium and actual reality reside.

But as long you allow the I-thought to lock your mind exclusively into the physical world of matter, you won't discover the Kingdom of Heaven within you.

Discussion Topic:

Imagine yourself in this dilemma: you're a parent whose child develops an inoperable brain-tumour, and the child is placed on a life-support system. After several weeks, consultant surgeons pronounce that your child is now 'brain-stem dead', and they require your permission to switch off the machine.

Would you give it?

If you would: why would you do this?

And if you wouldn't: why wouldn't you do this?

50

Psychological Fears and their Effects
Are you a slave of your subconscious mind?

If a child is born in France, it grows up learning to speak French; it'll be immersed in French culture and traditions, and in the laws of that country.

Environment plays a large, though not exclusive, part in our development as personalities.

If a child's beginnings are fraught with emotional instability, insecurity, and are devoid of love, he could develop deep psychological complexes which could cause him anguish for decades.

In our formative years, painful thoughts and feelings associated with a lack of love can quickly lead to a feeling of emotional instability and they can lodge easily within our subconscious minds, deep down, and there they can create a mental program or blueprint which, from then onwards, could govern much of our future thoughts, attitudes and behaviour patterns – until we learn to break these chains.

Guilt, fear, and feelings of inadequacy, which are frequently placed into young and plastic minds by unsuspecting guardians, can produce an adult who suffers either from depression or from a sense of worthlessness.

It's long been known that the subconscious mind is easily frightened and that it doesn't forget its powerful fears.

Indeed, we are creatures of habit.

If a puppy's cruel master beats it mercilessly with a stick he will cause it psychological or emotional damage. But if the same man teaches another pup that sticks are meant only to be thrown and retrieved (which produces cuddles from him, and great fun and loving praise) he will give this pup a sense of being loved, and this will encourage feelings of emotional security within its mind.

When the dogs mature, unsurprisingly the beaten dog will be terrified of sticks because its subconscious mind will never forget that sticks cause pain and anxiety.

We human beings have also been conditioned in this way, for deep within the mind everything is remembered and nothing is ever lost; and no experience is ever wasted.

Adults can very easily damage their children's emotions: a child's trust is so innocent that while developing its personality it seeks only to please its guardians. But adults often betray this trust; and I'm not referring to obvious malpractice such as physical or sexual abuse, but to everyday events which can make children believe they're 'surplus to requirements', 'unwanted', 'ugly', 'unlovable', or 'unworthy'.

Shockwaves created by such deep mental wounds as these can plague an individual right through his life and into old age, and they can even cross the divide with him when death occurs.

Parents can cause a child to suffer when they

fail to praise its efforts and, instead, harshly judge its results.

Here's a true story of what a few moments of adult thoughtlessness did to one human psyche:

To protect her identity I'll call my healing patient Jean. When she was about five years old Jean was admitted to hospital for a minor operation, and she was very frightened by the prospect. Her mother and father came to see her but they had to stand *outside* the ward doors; they weren't allowed at her bedside because of isolation procedures. But this wasn't explained to their sensitive daughter, who simply cried in despair as they waved to her from behind glass panels.

Jean couldn't understand why her mother and father didn't run to her and embrace her. She wanted to be hugged and told that she was loved and missed, and that she'd be all right.

She wanted to feel the warmth and closeness of her parents, or, at the very least, to be given an explanation of their behaviour – but none was forthcoming.

She was left in a state of anxiety, the emotional scars of which affect her life to this very day – and she's now in her seventies.

The young girl reasoned that if her parents didn't love her, then no one else would either. A powerful and deep rejection complex formed within Jean's young mind and since then, right throughout her life, she's felt 'unworthy of anyone's love'.

To this day, she remains fearful of forming loving relationships. Because her subconscious mind doesn't want to experience that painful sense of rejection again, whenever anyone tries to express love to her she runs away, *literally* – she usually takes an overseas holiday.

Jean remains an unhappy woman who longs for a husband or a lover at her side, but her early conditioning won't allow her to fulfil this desire.

She must, of course, break this circle of pain: and only she can do it.

All of this anguish was caused by people who didn't treat Jean with the understanding and respect that all children deserve of us: remember, we shouldn't only be their guardians, we should also be their best friends.

Even today, countless millions of people lack good parenting skills, despite the fact that this knowledge is available to everyone.

Perhaps you may recall similar happenings in your own life; if so: because you now understand the mechanisms involved, you can break their hold over you – for ever.

When your mind is set free from the ceaseless chattering of unnecessary painful thoughts and negative emotions and memories, at the core of your being you'll find a depth of healing peace.

Our levels of consciousness can be likened to a vast ocean: on the surface there is constant movement (tides incessantly ebb and flow and forever react to transient weather conditions), but deep down in the fathomless depths of our Selves the waters remain profoundly undisturbed. The essence of your spiritual being exists there in a state of healing stillness and tranquillity.

Whenever things go wrong we have a tendency to look outside ourselves and lay the blame at the feet of anyone but us. Very seldom do we accept full responsibility for our thoughts and actions.

For instance, if we feel unloved we often blame others for their lack of care, rather than ask ourselves, 'Why am I unloved? Is it because I've never shown love to others?'

Action and Reaction are both equal and opposite.

What we sow, we shall reap: the thoughts we put out into the Universe will eventually return to us — and often with greater force.

There are many ways of expressing spiritual truth, but there's only one way to develop and improve the quality of your soul — you have to work at it.

The Kingdom of Heaven is within you, waiting to be found.

Discussion Topic:

Think back to a time in your life when someone hurt you quite badly, either physically or emotionally.

Now examine your conscience and answer these questions truthfully:

Do you hold any bitterness in your heart against that person? (If you do: why do you?)

Have you tried to forgive that person? (If you haven't: why haven't you done this?)

51

Indifference to Emotion

If the truth of this next statement can be realised,
one of the main hurdles towards soul-growth may
be surmounted: *Don't be controlled by your
emotions; seek rather to be aware of them but not
to be dominated by them.*

Some spiritual advisors advocate cultivating a
sense of Detachment from disturbing emotions in
our psyches, but I disagree, for we can never
detach ourselves from the forces living within us.

Our feelings are an integral part of us: we are our
feelings, and they are us. Human beings are full of
sentience: we're not cold, unemotional creatures.

In order to progress spiritually, we should accept
the reality of every emotion living within us.

We cannot experience the welcome sensation of
pleasure without simultaneously admitting into
our hearts its intimate companion – pain. By fully
accepting the darker energies of emotion within us
(such as our hatred, anger, fear, ambition and
selfishness etc) we're accepting ourselves for what
we are, and not for what we feel we ought to be.

To deny your intrinsic feelings is to lie to
yourself, and this isn't a good foundation upon
which to build your spirituality, for truth can't

breathe the same air as hypocrisy.

However, we have the power to rise above the cloudy realms of emotional over-reaction that can so easily upset the delicate harmony of our bodies, minds and spirits. Instead of allowing negative emotions to turn us into their slaves, we can annihilate their effects through the realisation, and then the expressing, of the benign soul-quality of Indifference.

Indifference to emotion doesn't imply any loss of compassion on our part: by indifference I don't mean that we should no longer care about our feelings and emotions: I mean that we should be aware of our feelings (and those of others) in any situation, but not allow our emotions to interfere with our ability to take right and proper action.

If you wish to view this concept as a form of detachment, then so be it; but I would add to this idea the important qualification that we should *detach with love*.

An Indifferent man knows that whatever is taking place at any given time will happen anyway, no matter how he might feel about it.

In a life-or-death medical situation, an indifferent nurse is more capable of attending a wounded patient than an over-emotional novice is, for the novice's tears might prevent her from serving effectively.

Both nurses are compassionate, but I know which one I'd prefer to help me in such a crisis.

Spiritual people should always strive to love and serve others, but they shouldn't allow powerful emotions paralyse their ability to act.

Discussion Topic:

Your government passes a law stating that from tomorrow no butchers or slaughterhouse workers will ever be allowed to work in your country again.

From tomorrow, if you want to eat meat you must keep the animals yourself, then kill them, bleed them, skin them, and butcher them yourself.

Could you do this?

If you could; why could you?

And if you couldn't do this; why couldn't you?

PART FIVE

The Power of the Word

An Interview

51

An Interview with Stephen O'Brien
(Extracts from Psychic World *magazine, 2002, with questions put by John Sutton.)*

What was your first encounter with the spirit world?

I remember being visited by the spirit people when I was lying in my cot; I was about 18 months old. Lots of people came to see me and tickled me under my chin. A golden light surrounded some of these visitors, but it was only when I grew up that I realised they were not of this world.

Do you believe you have a spiritual mission in life?

Yes. I was born to spread the truth of eternal life to anyone who will listen; but I don't feel the need to be classified. I've been given many labels, but have rejected them all. Just as everyone else is, I'm a Child of God, and my religious ethics are these: to love and to serve.

Before I came into this world I promised the spirit people I'd help them in this mission, and I'm fulfilling this promise now.

Once my mission is achieved, you'll hear no more from me.

How do you intend to bring your message to the

world?

As well as through my books and articles, I've reached millions of souls via the media and the Internet. The worldwide web is a really big idea. Recently, a new community was founded (this is SOWIC, The Stephen O'Brien Worldwide Internet Community) and people are joining it in droves – they're logging on from all countries across the world.

We have members from as far afield as Alaska to New Zealand, Russia to Canada, right across Europe and the USA, and even in the Far and Middle East.

There's an online spiritual healing prayer book, too. All of the healing side of my work is done through the power of thought these days, because there are too many patients and only one of me.

But I'm only a channel, of course, a focal-point: God is the healer.

What role does your poetry and your books play in your life's work?

My poetry can best be described as metaphysical: it's the voice of one soul calling to another.

I'm a deeply private person, a lone individual, and I think my poetry reflects this sense of being stranded on Earth. Like *ET, The Extra-Terrestrial* in that magnificent film I'd like to go home; but I'll leave only when my work is done.

My books have helped and have given education and hope to many thousands, if not millions, of people. Some Spiritualists have criticised me for taking the spirit world's message into theatres on my UK tours, but that kind of narrow-mindedness doesn't bother me.

I was born with a vision, and I shall fulfil it. If someone doesn't like the picture I'm painting, that's fine by me. They too have the God-spark of Divinity within them, and they can paint their own pictures.

My books and teaching-recordings have been in print since 1989. Many thousands of souls and minds have been touched, and are still being encouraged to think for themselves. When you think about it: that's no mean achievement.

My work has made people think; it's brought them a little hope and some comfort, and it's also educated them on all manner of spiritual and psychic subjects.

And there's still more work for me to do. As the filmstar Mae West once said, 'I ain't dead yet!'

When you work in public how do you locate the recipients of your spirit messages?
Once I get in touch with a spirit communicator, it is he or she who finds the recipient, not I. I'm merely the channel.

I'm directed solely by my communicators, which is the way it should be; and I've never been satisfied with vague statements. I've always tried to get as much factual detail from them as possible, though I don't always succeed.

A medium's job is to present as much detailed evidence of survival as possible, and to serve those whose voices can no longer be physically heard.

In a public demonstration I concentrate on using clairaudience: I like to hear the spirit people. Clairaudients, I think, are more likely to receive accurate information.

How would you like to be remembered?
If people wish to recall me at all, then I'd like to think I'd be remembered for the work I did.

I find it frustrating when I read in some of today's psychic publications reports of mediumship meetings which simply state that 'good messages were relayed, and everyone had a lovely time.'

This is lazy journalism.

The detailed evidence of survival should be published: the actual words that the medium, the recipient, and the communicator said should be committed to print.

In many years from now someone will pick up these reports, and what will they see?

They need to know that survival has been proved, that spiritual healing has taken place, and that prophecies have been fulfilled.

We're a long way from everyone in the world accepting the reality of an afterlife, and the printed word can play an important part in pointing investigators in the right direction.

Do you do much work now with the media, i.e. TV and Radio?
I've kept the media at bay since 1995.

I still give a number of interviews, but much more rarely these days; and I pick and choose the offers with great care.

If people don't take my work seriously, then they don't get an interview.

It's as simple as that.

Far too many mediums seem desperate to jump on the publicity bandwagon.

Good luck to them; but there are the high levels of cynicism and downright rudeness in today's media.

And what is your attitude towards psychic researchers these days?

Many psychic researchers, parapsychologists and their like are... well, let's put it this way:

I can imagine a group of mediums and psychic researchers dying and, metaphorically speaking, being asked at the Gates of Heaven, 'And what did you do with your lives?'

Those who served would be let through and be given a pat on the back, and the others would be asked incredulously:

'Pardon? You mean to tell me that you spent your whole lives criticising other people's work, and you didn't even reach a sensible conclusion?'

I rest my case.

Having been in contact with spirit for many years what do you believe is the most important message you have to impart?

Love is eternal. Life is eternal. Love one another; care for one another. Don't fight and argue: reason matters out together.

Help those less fortunate than yourself.

Render service.

Be a peacemaker, not a militarist.

Bring peace into the world; and start that process now by first finding peace within yourself.

You are without doubt a very spiritual and gifted individual, so tell me Stephen O'Brien: in your opinion what is the meaning of life?
I see life as a crucible of experience.

We're born into this world to develop and grow in all aspects of our being: physically, emotionally, mentally, and spiritually.

No one is born by accident. God, The Great Spirit, breathes within all of us – which includes the creatures in the animal kingdom – and He's evolving through our experiences.

We're the vehicles that He has created, and through which he experiences His Universe. God is evolving continuously, and moving towards the bright Light of Love.

But many parts of Him are lagging way behind; and these are the parts of creation, the beings, whom many think of as evil or misguided.

By expressing our power of Love towards all creation, we are helping God to evolve.

How can people can learn more about you and your work, Stephen?
They can click on to the worldwide web, and join the psychic and spiritual mailing list to be kept up-to-date on all the new developments and the latest news.

You know, If I can make people think, then I've achieved my objective.

* * *

If you enjoyed this psychic book,
then you will enjoy reading Stephen O'Brien's
other bestselling titles,
and also listening to recordings of
his acclaimed spiritual and psychic teachings.

Books are available through all good Bookstores
and Libraries everywhere,
and signed copies are available from
the Voices Mail Order Service,
or via the Internet from
the Voices Online Shop at:
www.stephenobrien.co.uk

Full details, and a contact address for Stephen,
appear on the following pages.

Recommended Reading and Bibliography

This list contains a selection of educational and thought-provoking books that may help you to further your investigations.

They are listed by subject matter; and out-of-print titles may be obtained on the Internet or from specialist book-search companies. Your local library might also provide you with further information.

Teachings about the Spirit World:
The Spirit Speaks:
One of 10 philosophical books by the spirit guide 'Silver Birch', edited by Tony Ortzen. (Psychic Press Ltd: 1988)

Life in the World Unseen:
by Anthony Borgia. (Odhams Press & Psychic Press: c 1950)

Life After Life:
by Raymond Moody. (Bantam Books: 1975)

Children and Animals:
When your Child Dies: and *When your Animal Dies*:
both titles by Sylvia Barbanell. (Psychic Press: 1942-1970)

Children and the Spirit World:
by Linda Williamson. (Piatkus: 1997)

Children of the Light:
by Cherie Sutherland. (Souvenir Press: 1995)

Psychic Pets - the Secret World of Animals:
by Joseph Wylder. (New English Library: 1981)

Spiritual Conduct and Philosophy:
The Sufi Message:
by Hazrat Inayat Kahn. (International Headquarters of the Sufi Movement.) 14 books were published in India in 1989.

The Autobiography of a Yogi:
by Paramahansa Yogananda. (Rider Books: 1969)

Freedom from the Known:
by Krishnamurti. (Victor Gollancz 1969)

The Quiet Mind:
by White Eagle. (The White Eagle Publishing Trust: 1972)

The Garden of the Beloved:
by Robert Way. (Sheldon Press, London: 1975)

Words to Love By:
Spoken by Mother Teresa. (Walker & Company, NY: 1984)

Jonathan Livingston Seagull:
by Richard Bach. (Pan: 1972)

The Great Philosophers (from Socrates to Turing):
By Ray Monk and Frederic Raphael. (Phoenix Books: 2001)

Think:
By Simon Blackburn. (Oxford University Press: 1999)

The Ethics of Aristotle:
(Penguin Classics: 1953-1965)

A Discourse on the Method and *The Meditations*
by René Descartes (Penguin: 1968)

Spiritualism, the New Religion:
The Rock of Truth:
by Arthur Findlay. (Psychic Press Ltd: 1976)

Physical Mediumship:
The Story of Helen Duncan:
by Alan E Crossley. (Arthur H Stockwell Ltd: 1975)

The Case of Helen Duncan:
by Maurice Barbanell. (Psychic Press Ltd: 1945)

The Mediumship of Jack Webber:
by Harry Edwards. (Healer Publishing Co Ltd: 1962)

Voices in the Dark:
By Leslie Flint. (Psychic Press: 1988)

They Walked Among Us: (Physical medium, Alec Harris.)
by Louie Harris. (Psychic Press: 1980)

Spiritual Healing:
A Guide to the Understanding &
Practice of Spiritual Healing:
by Harry Edwards. (Healer Publishing Co. Ltd: 1974)

Spirit Healing:
By Harry Edwards. (Healer Publishing Co. Ltd: 1960)
(This author has written many other informative titles.)

Mind to Mind:
by Betty Shine. (Corgi: 1990)
(There is a whole series of books by this author.)

I Hear a Voice:
(Biography of EG Fricker, the Healer)
by Maurice Barbanell. (Spiritualist Press: 1962)

The Power of the Rays: (The Science of Colour-Healing)
By SGJ Ouseley. (LN Fowler Ltd: 1951-1986)

Let's Eat Right to Keep Fit
by Adelle Davis. (Unwin: 1954 – 1979) (Nutrition Therapy.)

Mediumship, and Mediumship Classics:
Mediumship Made Simple:
by Ivy Northage. (Psychic Press: 1986)

All About Mediumship:
by Ursula Roberts. (Two Worlds: 1994)

Fifty Years a Medium:
by Estelle Roberts. (Corgi: 1975)

Mediums and the Afterlife:
by Linda Williamson. (1992, Robert Hale)

Mediums and Their Work:
by Linda Williamson. (Robert Hale: 1990)

Voices in My Ear:
by Doris Stokes. (Futura: 1980)

On Life After Death:
By Elisabeth Kübler-Ross. (Celestial Arts, California, 1991)

Through the Mists:
by Robert James Lees. (Robert James Lees Trust: 1975)

The Projection of the Astral Body:
by Sylvan Muldoon & Hereward Carrington. (Rider: 1968)

Where Two Worlds Meet:
by Arthur Findlay. (Psychic Press: 1951)

Ena Twigg - Medium:
by Ena Twigg & Ruth Hagy Brod. (Hawthorn Books: 1972)

The Boy Who Saw True:
Author unknown - The psychic diary of an anonymous lad,
recorded from 1885-1927. (C W Daniel & Co Ltd: 1961)

*Visions of Another World; Voices from Heaven; In Touch
with Eternity; Angels By My Side; A Gift of Golden Light;
The Spiritual Keys to the Kingdom*:
by Stephen O'Brien.
(New Editions published by Voices Books: 1998-2002)

The Real Jesus of Nazareth?:
Jesus and The Goddess:
(Was Jesus an actual historical personality?)
by Timothy Freke and Peter Gandy. (Thorsons: 2002)

The Dead Sea Scrolls Deception:
by Michael Baigent and Richard Leigh. (Corgi Books: 1992)

The Passover Plot:
by Hugh J Schonfield. (McDonald/Futura 1965 and 1977)

The Miracles of Jesus:
by H J Richards. (Fontana: 1975)

The Gospel of the Essenes:
by Edmond Bordeaux Szekely. (C W Daniel & co Ltd : 1979)

The Childhood of Jesus, and also *The Manhood of Jesus*:
by Geraldine Cummings. (Psychic Press Ltd: 1972 & 1963)

The Gospel of Thomas:
by Hugh McGregor Ross. (Element Books: 1991)

The Psychic Life of Jesus:
by Revd G Maurice Elliott. (Psychic Press: 1948)

Psychic Portraiture (Psychic Art):
The Living Image:
by Coral Polge. (Thorsons; and Regency Press 1986)
Later republished as *Living Images*.

The Aura and Chakras:
The Raiment of Light:
by David Tansley. (Routledge & Kegan Paul Ltd: 1984)

The Human Aura:
by W J Kilner. (Weiser: 1984)
Originally published in 1911 as *The Human Atmosphere*.

(Also read books on Kirlian Photography.)

Working With Your Chakras:
By Ruth White. (Piatkus: 1993)

Reincarnation and Past Lives:
Eyes of Horus:
by Joan Grant. (Corgi: 1975)
(This author has written a series of books about her
previous lives)

The Search for Omm Sety:
by Jonathan Cott. (Rider Books: 1987)

In Touch with Eternity:
by Stephen O'Brien. (Voices Books: 2000)

Simple Self-Analysis and Psychology:
Prescription for Anxiety: (Overcome fear and depression)
by Leslie D. Weatherhead. (Abingdon: 1979)

Principles of Psychology:
by William James. (Dover Publications: 1955)

---

*This list is not definitive, but is meant to provide a general
introduction to some of the subjects covered in this book.*

Useful Addresses

The following organisations and societies might be able to help you with the development of your sensitivity. Their locations were correct at the time of printing, but check the Internet to obtain their current details and e-mail addresses.

A search on the worldwide web might prove helpful in locating similar groups and societies in your own country.

Many of these groups hold teaching-seminars and also provide psychic development facilities and workshops, as well as private consultations, healing courses, and the opportunity to witness public services of mediumistic and psychic work with well-known demonstrators. (These addresses are not listed in any particular order.)

College of Psychic Studies 16 Queensberry Place, London SW7 2EB.

Greater World Christian Spiritualist Association, 3-5 Conway Street, London W1T 6BJ.

Institute of Spiritualist Mediums, c/o Secretary, 121 Church End Lane, Runwell, Wickford, Essex, SS11 7DN.

International Spiritualist Federation, c/o Secretary, PO Box 25282, London, N12 7WY

The Lynwood Fellowship, Royes Ridge, Plough Hill, Caistor, Lincoln, LN7 6UR.

The Noah's Ark Society for Physical Mediumship, c/o Secretary, 7 Sheen Close, Grange Park, Swindon, Wiltshire, SN5 6JF.

Spiritualist Association of Great Britain,
33 Belgrave Square, London SW1X 8QB.

Spiritualists' National Union, The Arthur Findlay College,
Stansted Hall, Stansted, Mountfitchet, Essex, CM24 8UD.

White Eagle Lodge, New Lands. Brewells Lane, Rake, Liss,
Hampshire, GU33 7HY.

The Sue Rowlands Centre, at Tre-Ysgawen Hall,
Capel Coch, Llangefni, Anglesey, North Wales, LL77 7UR.

Psychic News, The Coach House, Stansted Hall, Stansted,
Essex CM24 8UD. (Weekly Spiritualist/Psychic newspaper.)

Psychic World, PO Box 14, Greenford, Middlesex,
UB6 0UF. (Monthly Spiritualist/Psychic magazine.)

Two Worlds, A3 Riverside, Metropolitan Wharf,
Wapping Wall, London, E1W 3SS.
(Monthly Spiritualist/Psychic magazine.)

Overseas
Greater World Christian Spiritualist Association,
3-5 Conway Street, London WI P 5HA, UK.
(The association has affiliated churches in Northern
Ireland, The Channel Islands, Australia, Canada, Nigeria
and South Africa.)

National Spiritualists' Association Churches, c/o Secretary,
PO Box 217, Lily Dale, New York 14752, USA.

Spiritualist Alliance (Auckland) Inc., PO Box 9477,
Newmarket, Auckland 1, New Zealand

There are psychic societies, groups and organisations in
practically every country in the world, and most of these are
represented on the worldwide web – so search the Internet
for further information.

Books by Stephen O'Brien

'THE SPIRITUAL KEYS TO THE KINGDOM'
A Book of Soul-Guidance for your Life,
by Stephen O'Brien.

Priceless Wisdom and Guidance
to Help you Throughout your Life

- Unlock the Secrets of Eternity
- Unfold the Hidden Psychic Powers of your Soul
- Discover the Kingdom of Heaven within you
- Obtain Happiness and Peace of Mind.
- Dip into this Treasure-Chest of Guidance Each Day - Be Uplifted and Receive all the Inspiration you need.

You are the Traveller walking along Life's Ancient Pathway, seeking answers to your questions and trying to fathom the meaning of your existence. As you step into the Mystical Valley of Wisdom, Angelic Beings of Light speak to your mind and heart, and they hand to you *The Spiritual Keys to the Kingdom* which will help you to develop your natural spiritual powers, generate health in your body, mind and spirit, increase your sense of happiness and contentment, and understand your life-purpose and why you were born.

Seven years in the making, this enthralling book contains the wisdom of some remarkable Spiritual Voices recorded by the world-renowned visionary, Stephen O'Brien. They will speak to you of hope and love, and of everlasting life, and will reveal to you the future of your soul.

A Voices Paperback Original (384 pages)
ISBN: 0-9536620-5-5

'VISIONS OF ANOTHER WORLD'
The Autobiography of a Medium,
by Stephen O'Brien.

Every Journey has a Beginning...

Phantom hands hammering on a door
in the dead of night:
THE SPIRIT WORLD WAS CALLING...
and Stephen O'Brien had to accept the remarkable
powers that brought him *Visions of Another World.*
Then the tragic early death of his mother broke his
life in two; but miraculously she appeared to him
from beyond the grave
and her love changed the course of his life:
he became a Medium and a Visionary.
He promised the soul of a long-dead American Indian
that he would serve the Spirit World,
and countless thousands packed out venues
to hear him relay messages of Hope,
Light and Survival
from their loved ones on the Other Side of Life.
Hundreds of thousands of the so-called 'dead' have
now communicated through Stephen O'Brien's
amazing gifts: including war heroes,
accident and murder victims,
innocent children who died too young, animals,
and even the world-famous actress, Judy Garland.
Now you can read Stephen's compelling life-story.

'Big powers in other-worldly communication
and healing' *Irish News*

A Voices Paperback (384 pages; illustrated)
ISBN: 0-9536620-3-9

'ANGELS BY MY SIDE'
The Psychic Life of a Medium,
by Stephen O'Brien.

'We are not alone in this Universe...'

Stephen O'Brien's extraordinary spiritual and
psychic gifts have comforted millions of people and
have silenced sceptics around the world.
In *Angels By My Side* Stephen reveals through his
acclaimed powers:

- Timeless Wisdom from the 'Silent Sentinels'
  and Angel Beings who watch over us.
- Fascinating glimpses into Mankind's Future.
- The secret Psychic Powers of Light and Colour that
  enhance Wellbeing and Self-healing.
- A compelling view of 'The One Living God'.
- What kind of life awaits us all after death,
  and the secrets of the Next World.
- Irrefutable Evidence of Survival.

He also shares with his countless readers
more of his amazing Out-of-the-Body Excursions
into the Spirit World itself.

A Voices Paperback (384 pages; illustrated)
ISBN: 0-9536620-0-4

'IN TOUCH WITH ETERNITY'
Contact with Another World,
by Stephen O'Brien.

*'As the hazy shape materialised
there was revealed to us an Angel of Light,
a beautiful woman with golden hair,
whose eyes were deep blue-green like
unfathomed ocean waters.
'Peace,' she said...'*

Make incredible journeys into the World of the Spirit
with Stephen O'Brien's remarkable
True-Life Psychic Experiences:
Go behind the scenes at Séances and discover how
Guardian Angels strive to contact us through the
Psychic Power that we unknowingly provide.
Read stunning Survival Evidence of human and
animal souls after death, including children's
messages to their parents and a communication
from Dr Martin Luther King.

- Unveil the truth about Reincarnation, Telepathy,
  Life Before Life, Out-of-the-Body Experiences,
  Soul Powers, and how to Heal with Psychic Sound.
- Encounter *'The Shining Ones'* deep within the
  Spiritual Spheres of Light, and learn of their
  concern for the human family and for our planet.
- Meet the Nature Spirits, and some amazing
  Animals that can communicate with us.

A Host of Fascinating Spiritual Experiences
from Britain's Renowned Visionary,
Medium and Healer.

A Voices Paperback (352 pages; illustrated)
ISBN: 0-9536620-2-0

'VOICES FROM HEAVEN'
Communion with Another World,
by Stephen O'Brien.

Grieving parents are reunited with their children,
wives with their husbands, and even animals return
to prove what medium Stephen O'Brien affirms:
'*Death is only an Illusion.*'
Follow Stephen as he makes remarkable journeys
into the Realms of Light and discovers the Eternal
World of the Spirit that awaits us all after 'death'.
In these fascinating psychic recollections
the world-renowned visionary reveals to his countless
followers many remarkable life-changing and
spiritual experiences, during which he:

- ❖ Crosses Time-Zones and meets people who are
  long-dead.
- ❖ Relays startling messages from screen goddess
  Marilyn Monroe, from Lord Olivier, and from
  Earl Mountbatten of Burma.
- ❖ Foresees the *Challenger* Space Shuttle disaster,
  an incredible five years before it happened.
- ❖ Provides irrefutable evidence of the immortality
  of the soul.

*

And the Angel's Voice said:
'The road is never spiritually lonely,
and we will not forsake you.
We will guide and bless you, for ever...'

'The epitome of mediumistic excellence' –
Psychic News

A Voices Paperback (384 pages; illustrated)
ISBN: 0-9536620-4-7

'A GIFT OF GOLDEN LIGHT'
The Psychic Journeys of a Medium,
by Stephen O'Brien.

*(If you are interested in developing your own
psychic or spiritual powers, simply by reading this
book you will learn all the important lessons and
guidelines that Stephen learned during his long
apprenticeship.)*

The press described this remarkable book as
'un-put-downable'.

Follow Stephen as he recalls his exciting 20-year
psychic apprenticeship and strives to perfect the
extraordinary paranormal skills which have brought
happiness, comfort and hope to millions of people.
With warmth and candour he:

♦ Shares his thrilling encounters with Apparitions,
  Hauntings, Spiritual Healing and Telepathic
  Powers.
♦ Reveals the mystical Gift of Golden Light which
  illuminates everyone's Spiritual Journey through
  Life.
♦ Presents a compelling array of Survival Evidence
  of Human and Animal Souls after death.

'Stunning clairvoyance... superb mediumship' –
Psychic News

A Voices Paperback (384 pages; illustrated)
ISBN: 0-9536620-1-2

Keep in touch with our mail order department for
news of new titles and other products
originated by Stephen.

The Spoken Word:
Six Recordings by the Same Author.

High quality digital stereo recordings,
running-time 60 minutes each, containing a wealth of
information and education that all seekers, healers,
mediums and psychic readers should know.
Stephen O'Brien's gentle voice can speak in your
home or private development class, teaching and
explaining each subject in easy-to-understand terms.

Develop your Mediumship and Psychic Powers:
*A step-by-step guide to the unfoldment and
safe practice of your psychic and mediumistic skills.*

Heal Yourself:
*Gain peace of mind and freedom from stress.
The way to spiritual, physical, emotional and mental
self-healing and wellbeing; includes meditations.*

4 Meditations:
*Obtain peace & tranquillity; health & strength;
guidance & inspiration; sensitivity & awareness.*

Develop your Healing Powers:
*Everyone's guide to success as a healer.
'We all have the power to heal.'*

4 Visualisations:
*Relax your body; calm your mind;
quieten your spirit; refresh your soul.*

Life After Death:
*What awaits the soul after its transition.
Life in the World of Spirit is revealed.*

By mail order from the Voices Online Shop at
www.stephenobrien.co.uk

For further information on all aspects of the
life and work of visionary, spiritual healer,
medium and poet, Stephen O'Brien,
including how to obtain by Mail Order
his bestselling books, educational recordings,
spiritual healing crystals, and a full range of
other quality products (or to contact him directly)
please write, enclosing a large SAE, to:

VOICES MANAGEMENT
(Dept VB7)
PO Box 8
SWANSEA
SA1 1BL
UK

Or search the Internet for 'Stephen O'Brien'.
Visit our Online Shop where you may order signed
copies of all of the Stephen O'Brien products at:
www.stephenobrien.co.uk

Voices Management regrets it cannot reply
without a large stamped self-addressed envelope
and correspondents are respectfully advised
not to mail irreplaceable items to the author,
for neither Voices, nor Mr O'Brien,
can accept responsibility for the loss or damage
of any unsolicited manuscripts, poems,
sentimental objects, photographs, or recordings etc.,
which are often posted by the public.
Your letters are always welcome,
but please keep them brief and to the point –
and be patient when awaiting your replies,
for Stephen receives vast quantities of mail
from around the world.

Thank you.